LET'S COLOR ANIMALS!

Another Coloring Book for Grown-Ups

By Jack Matirko

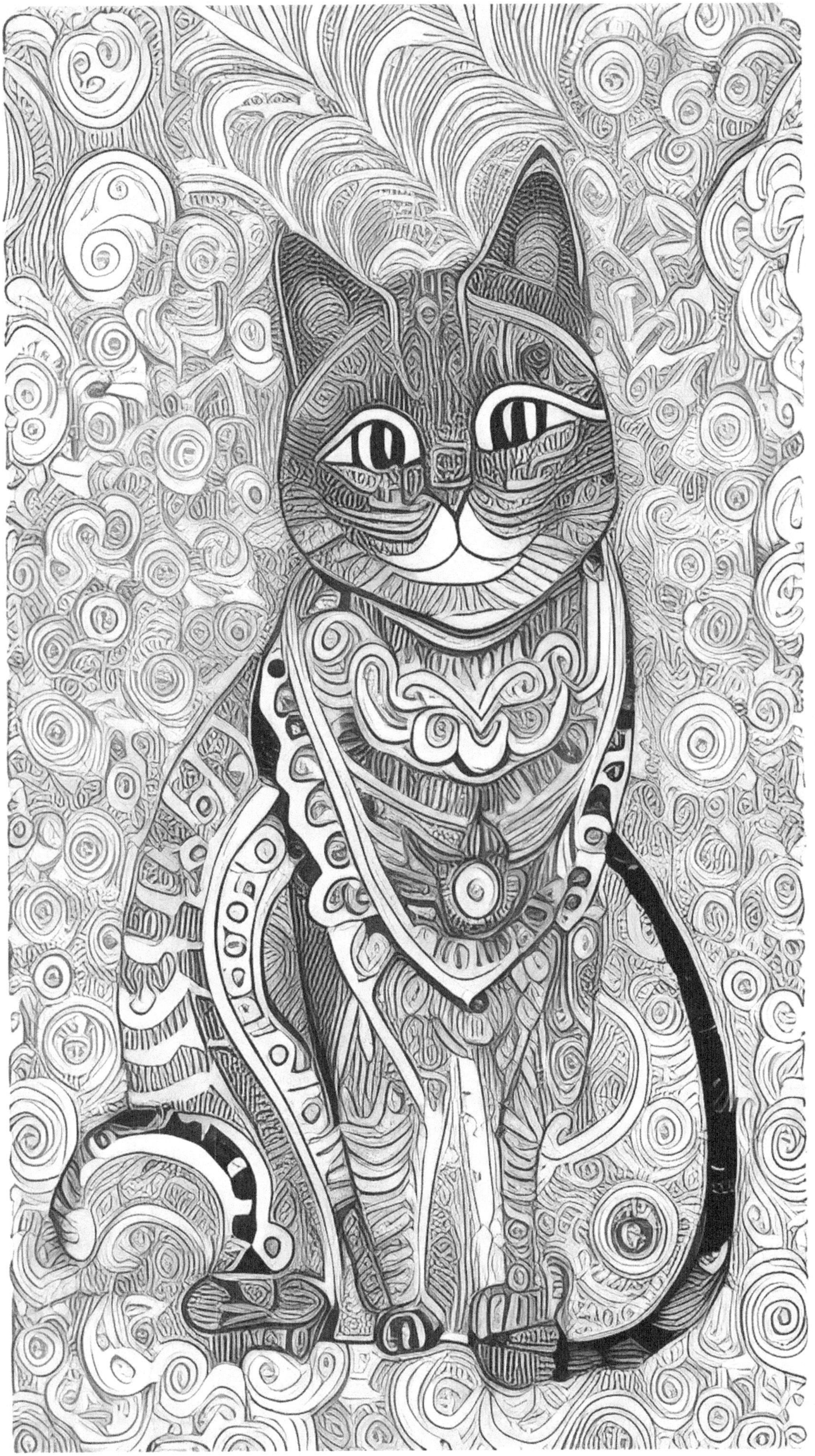

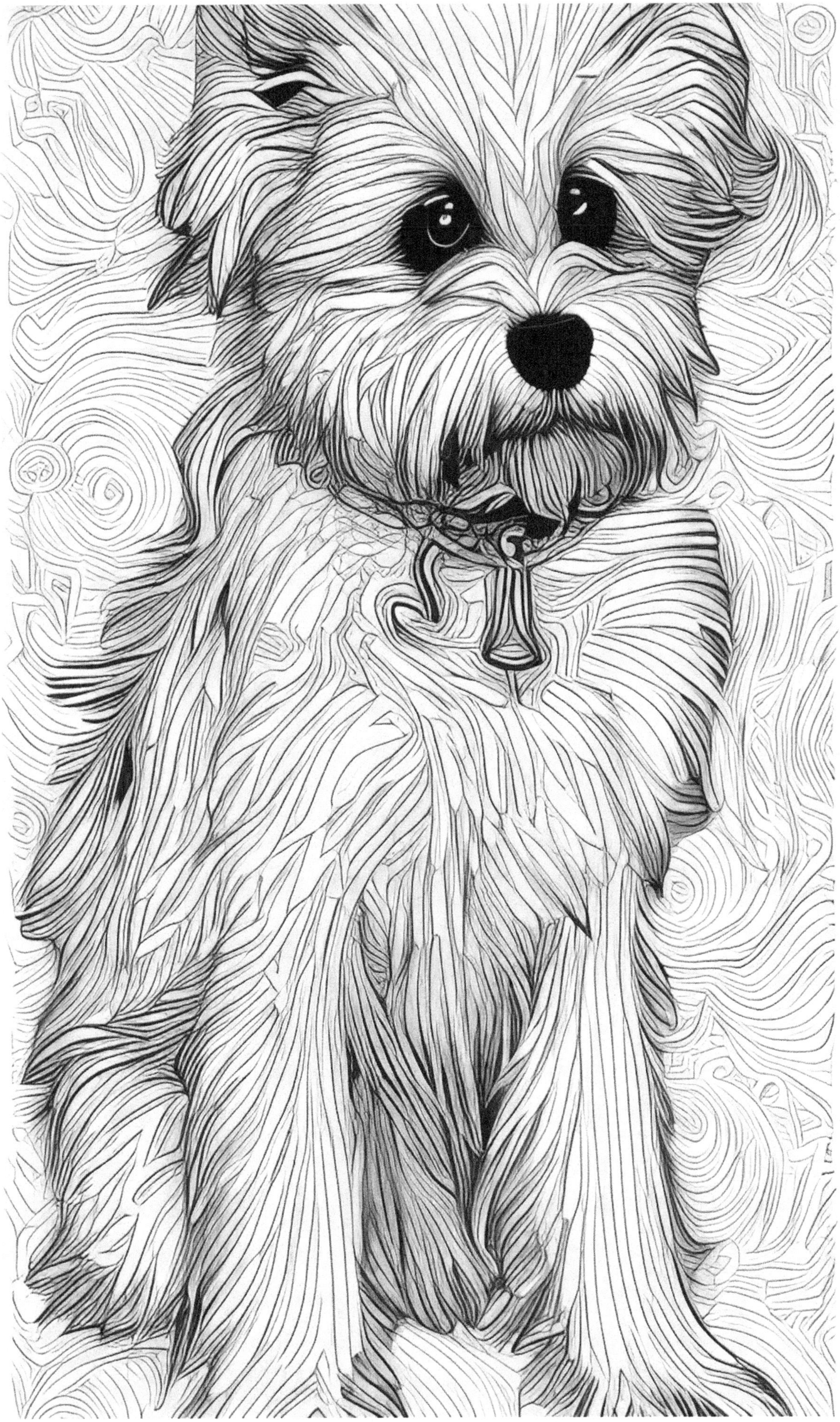

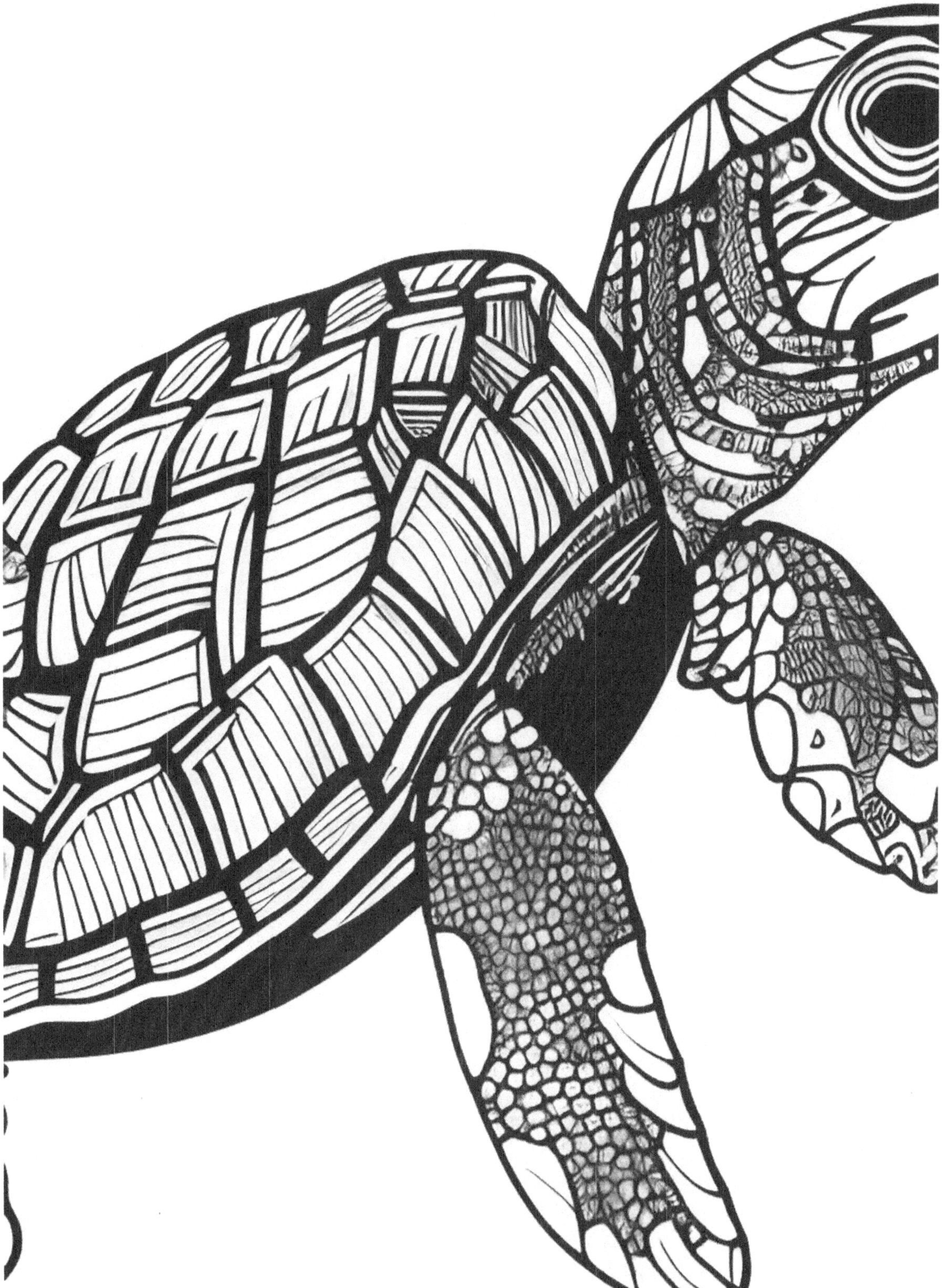

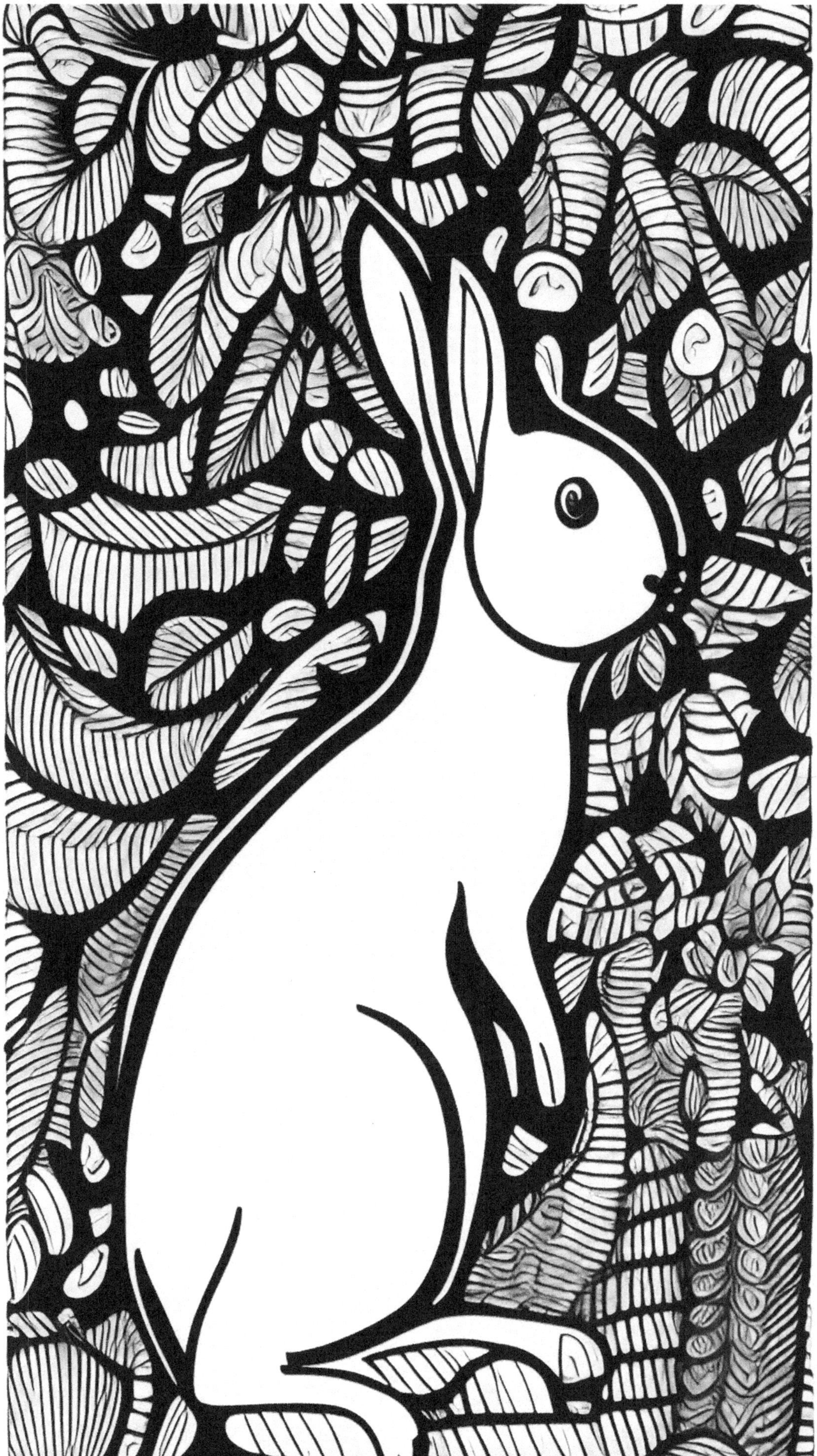

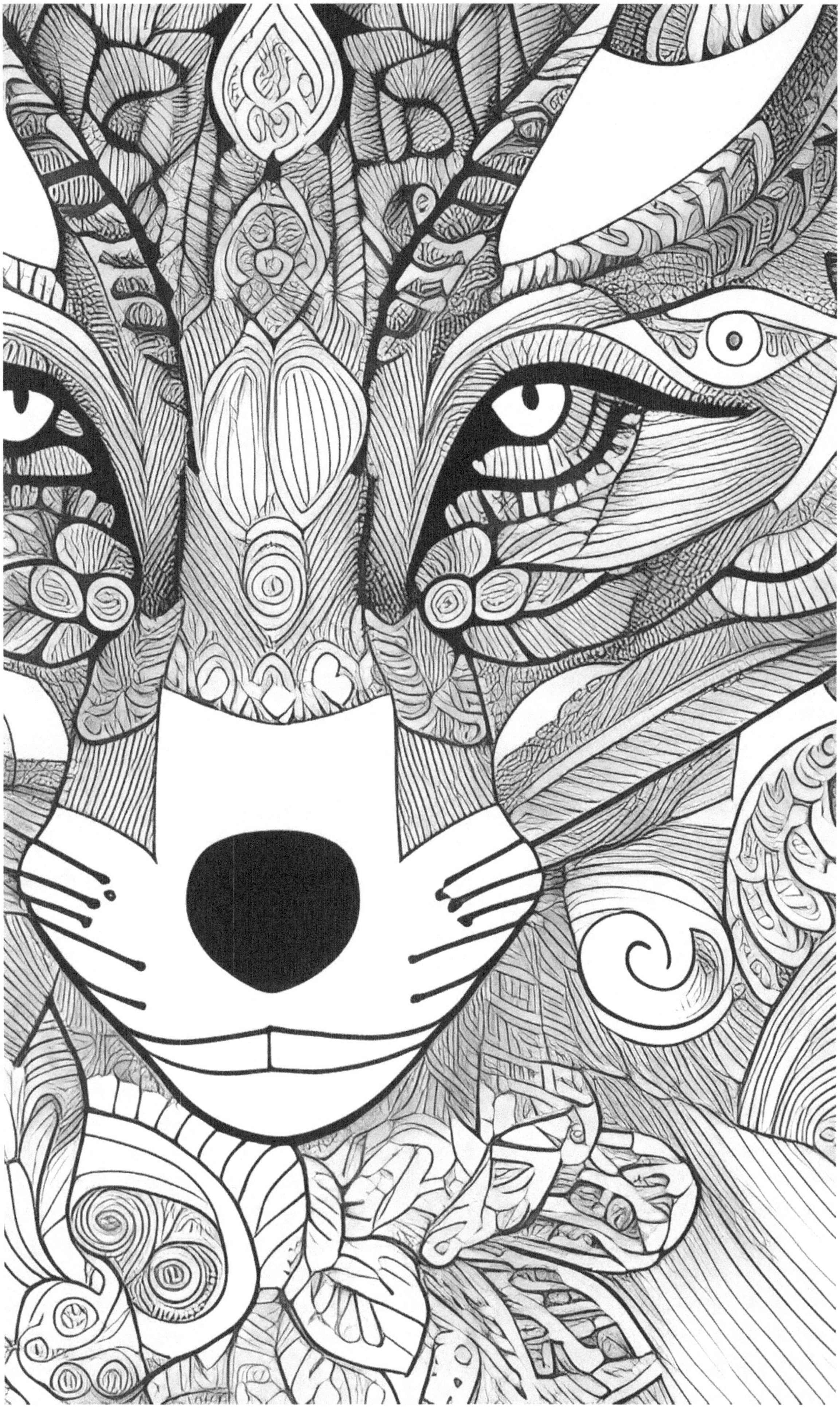

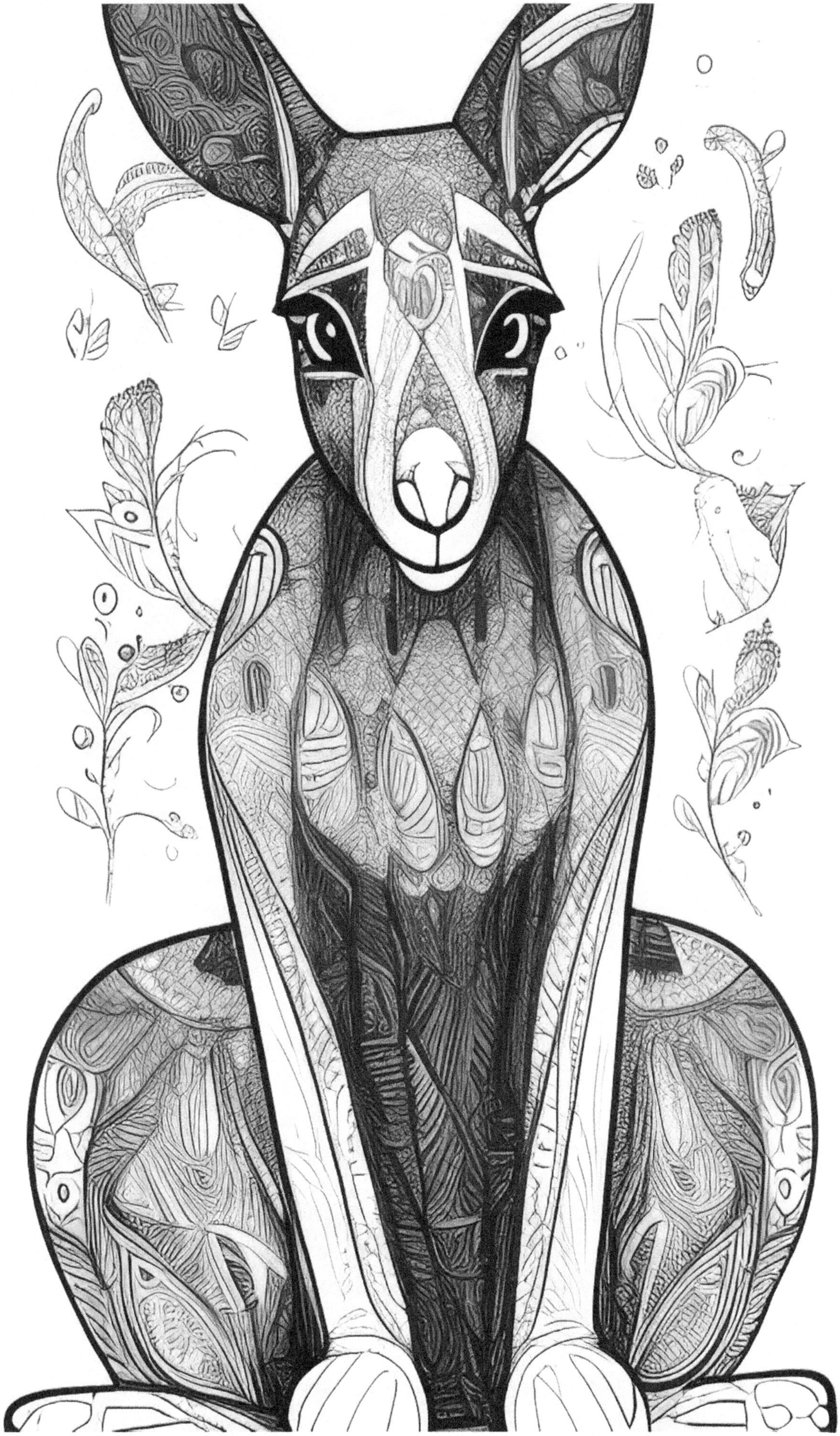

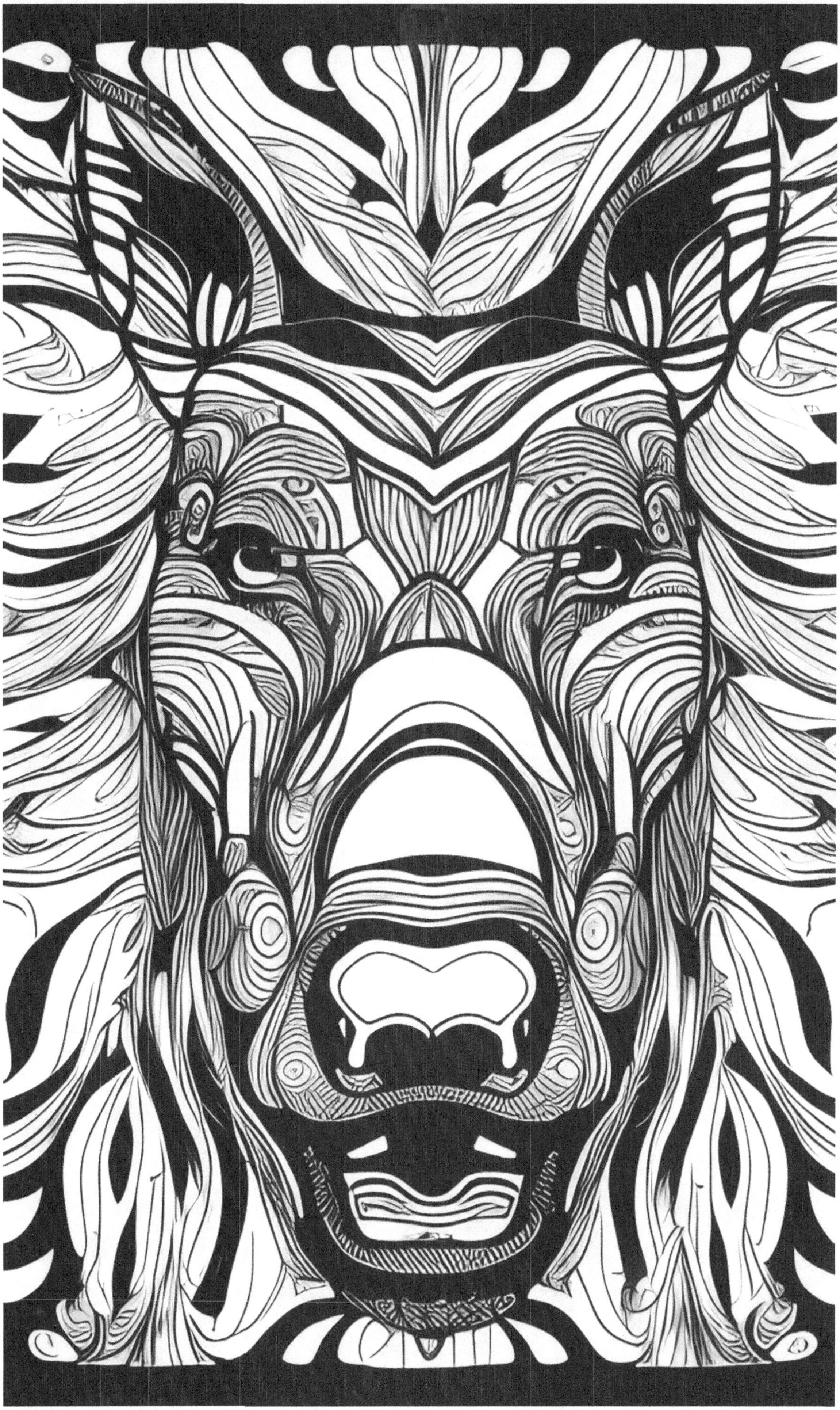

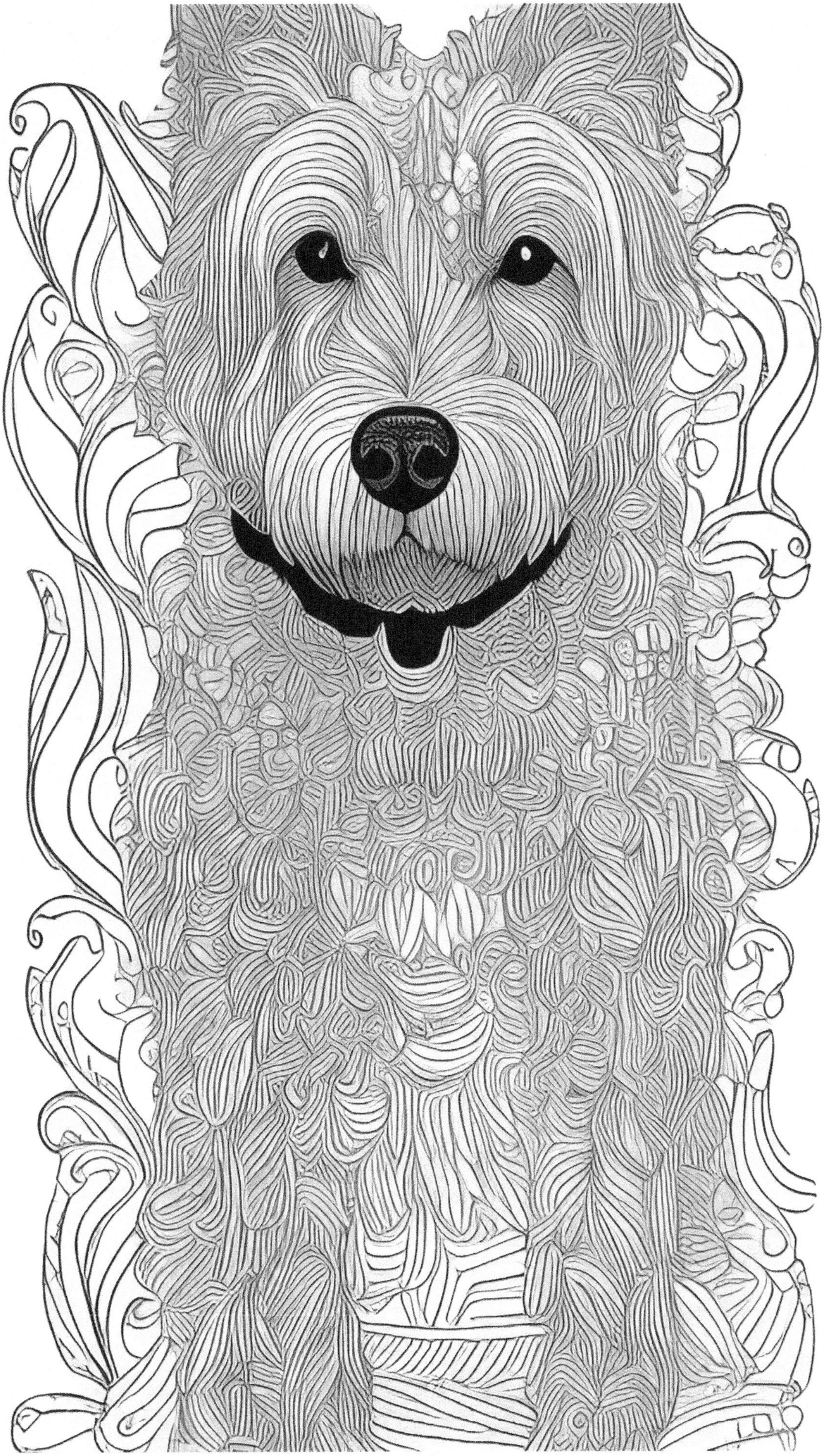

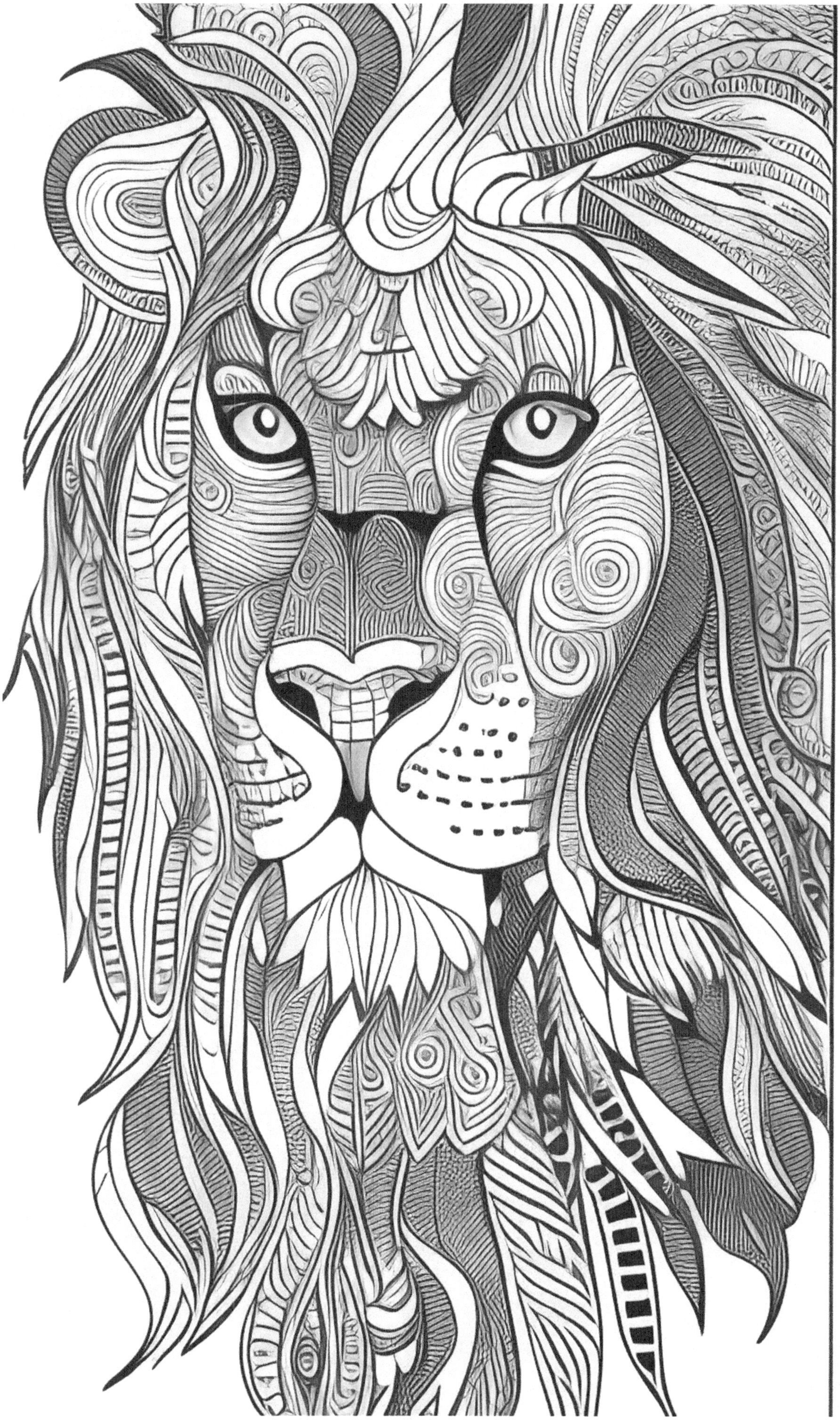

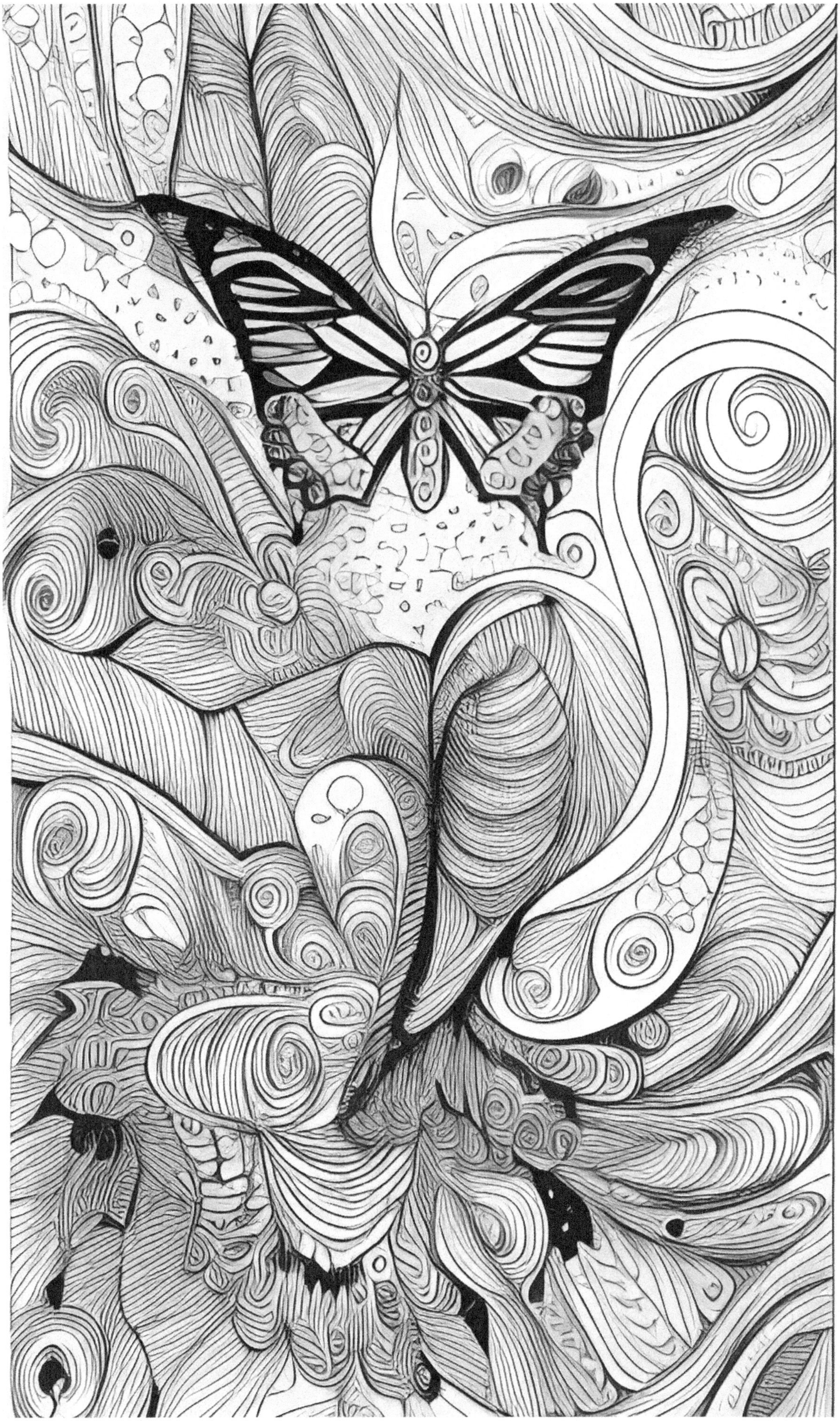

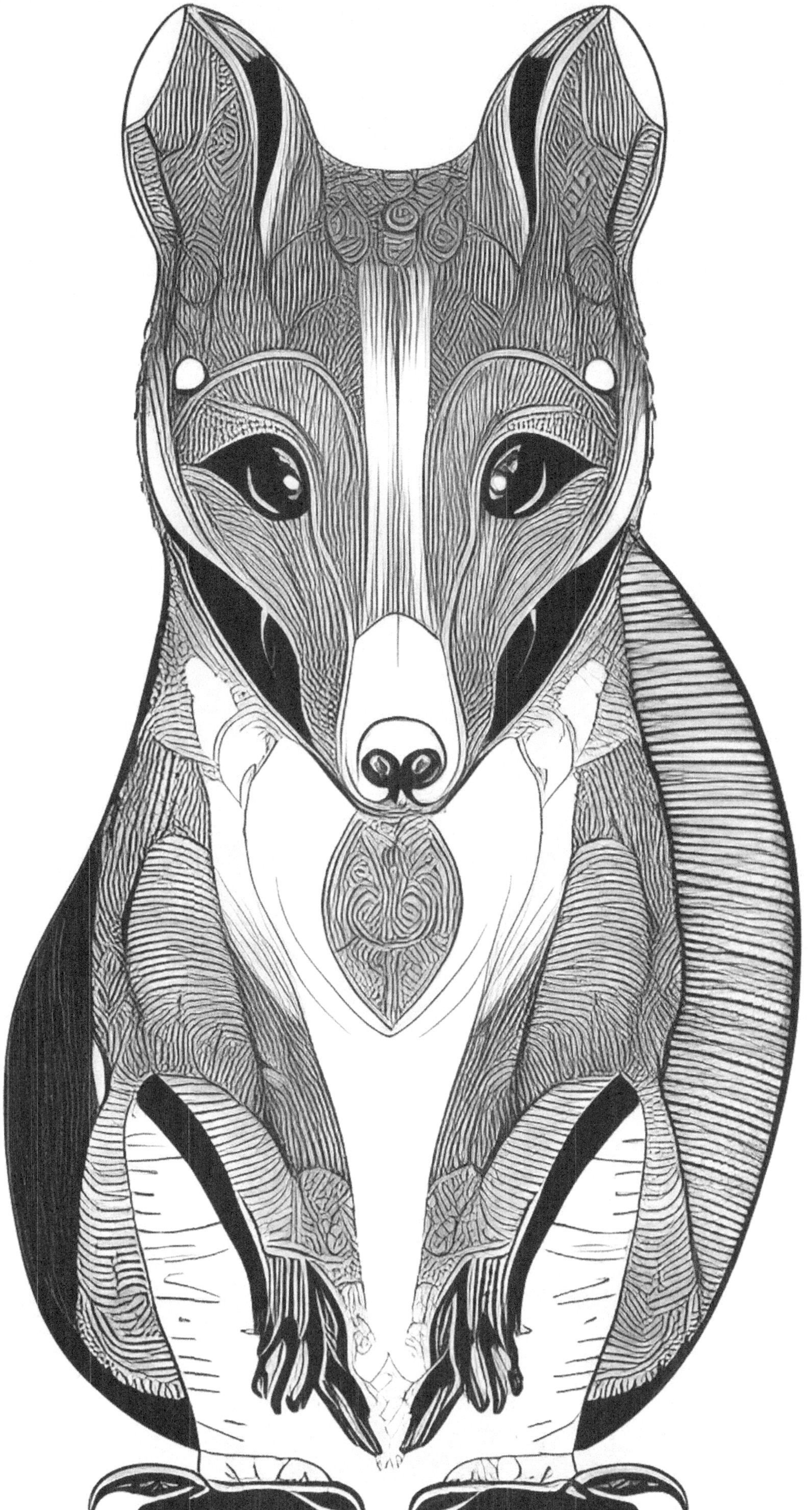

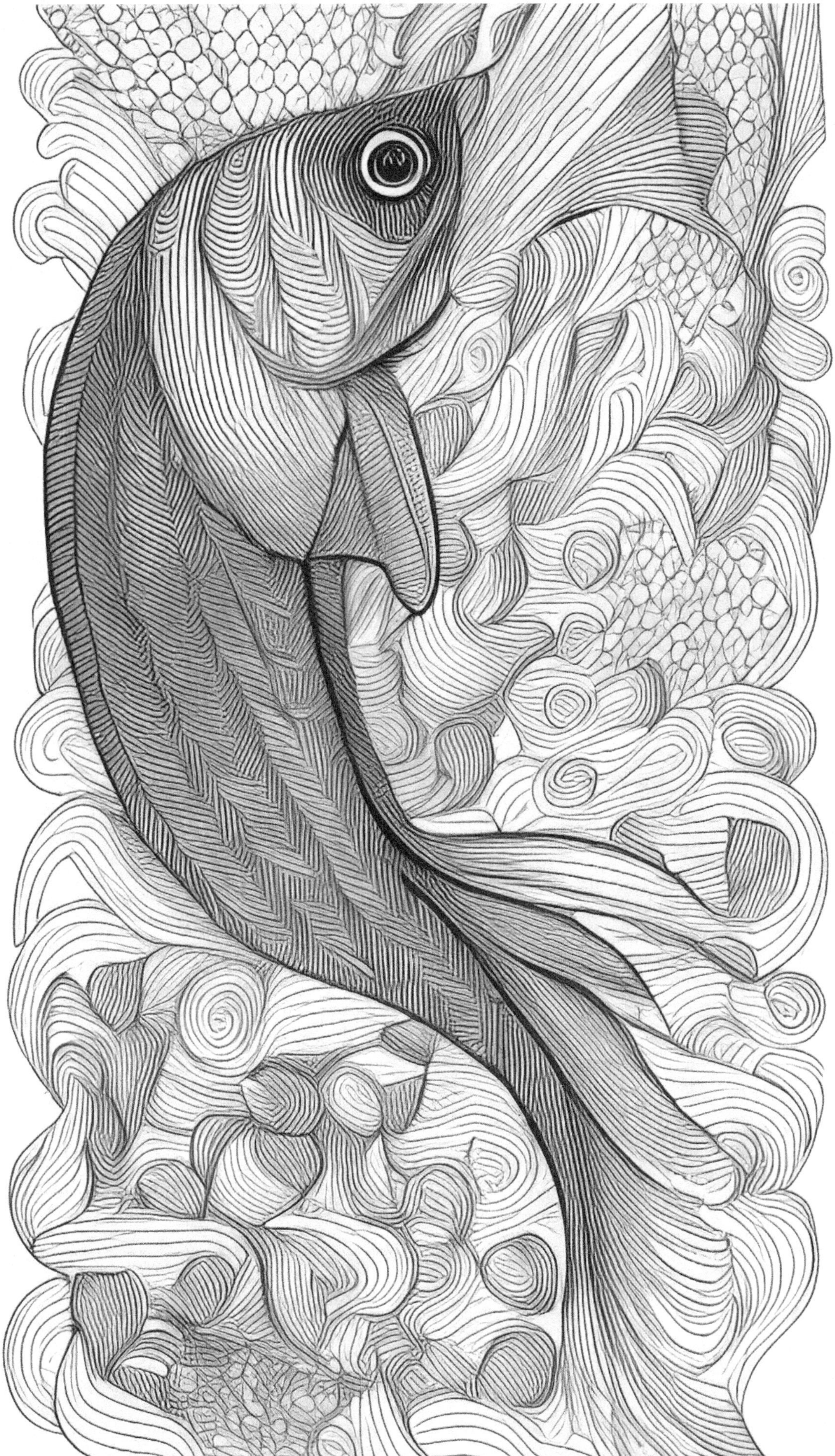

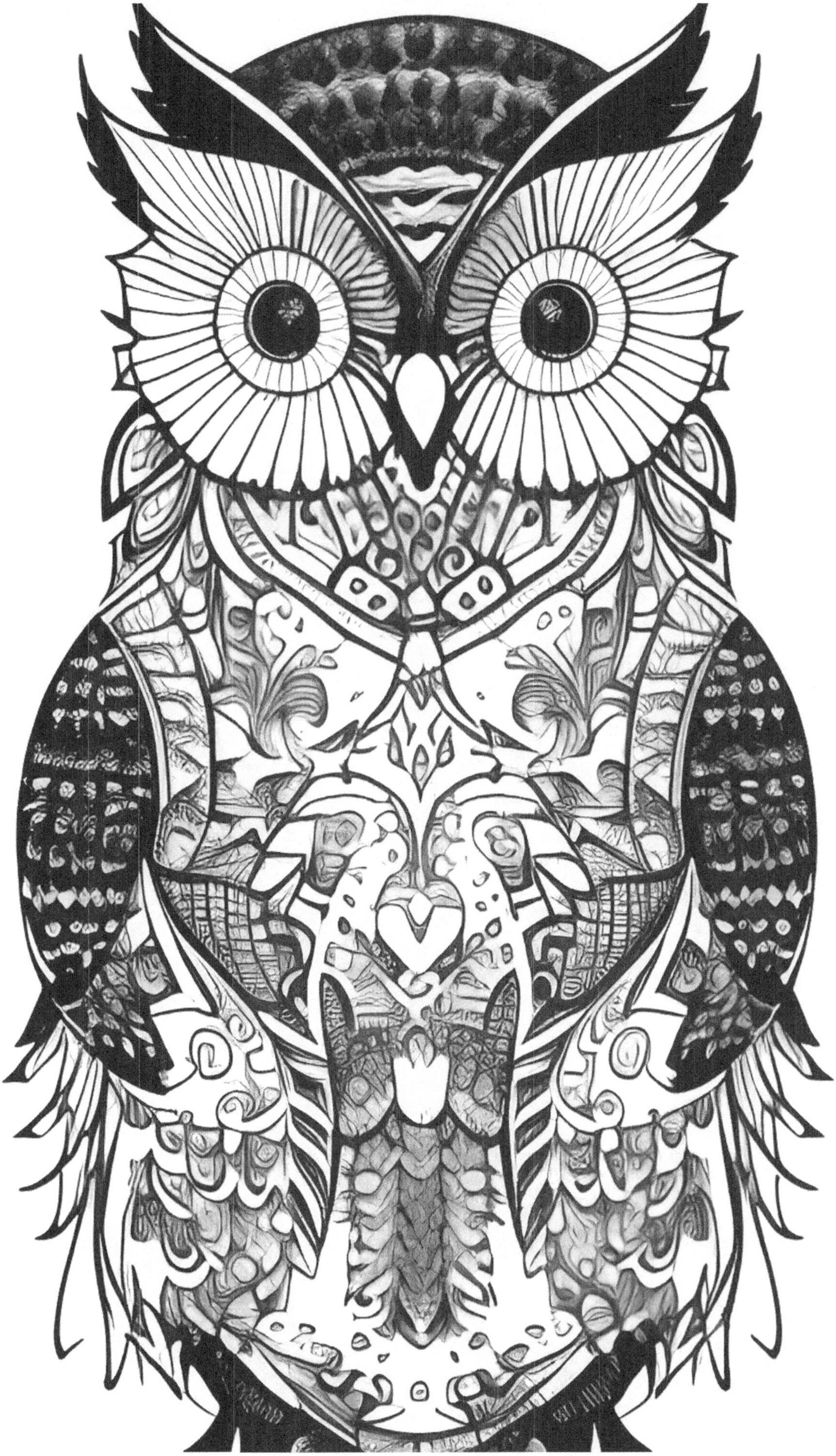

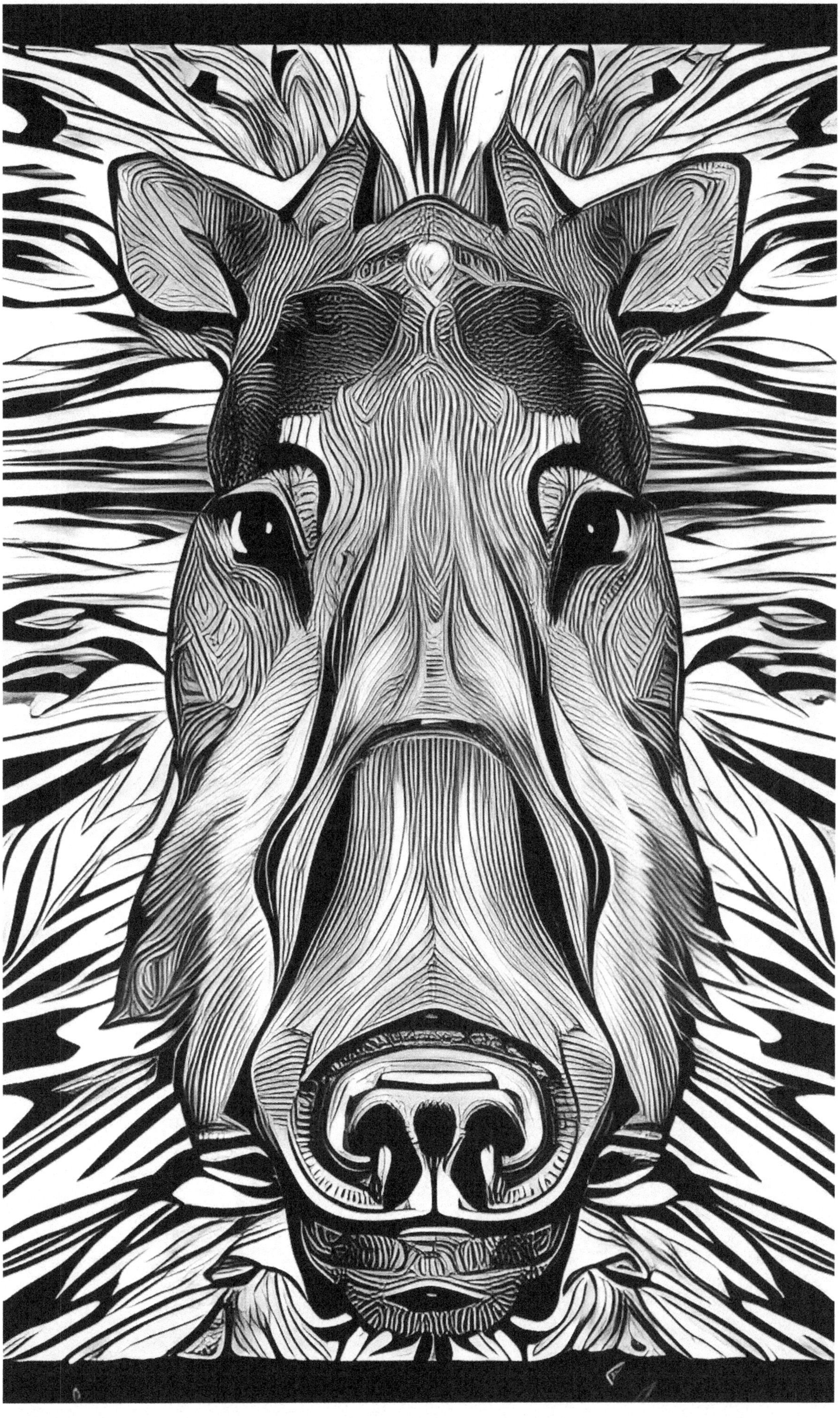

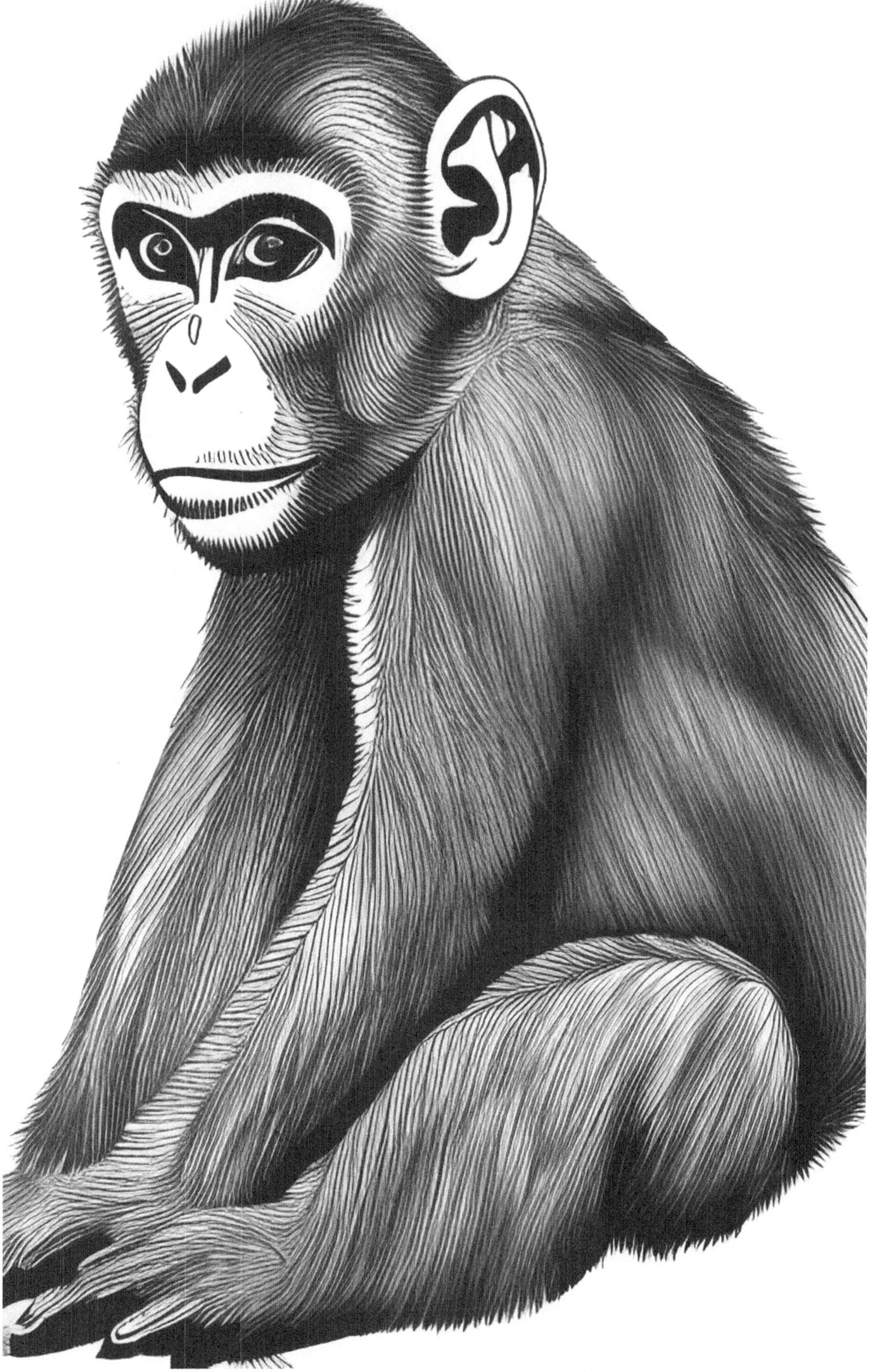

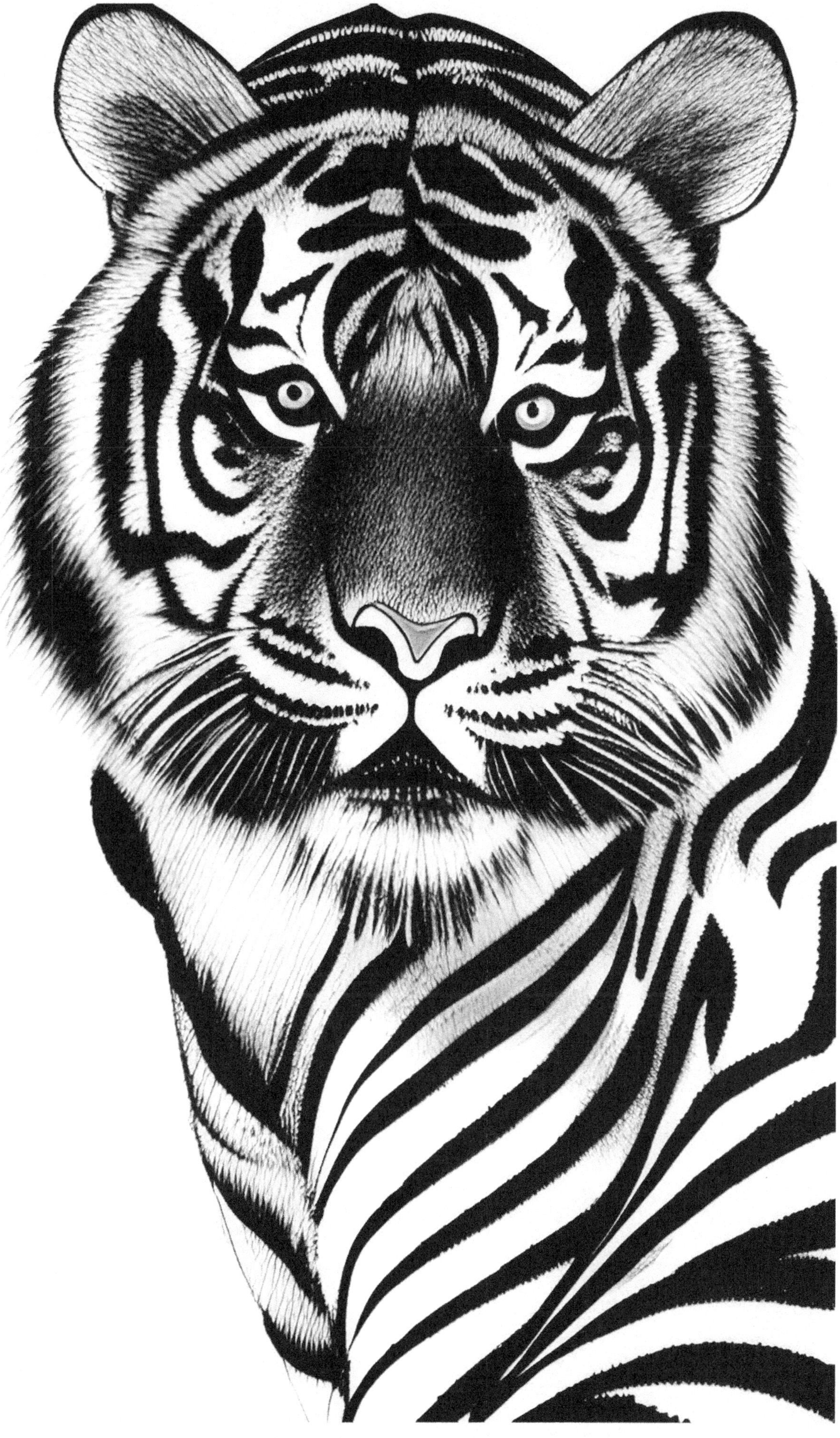

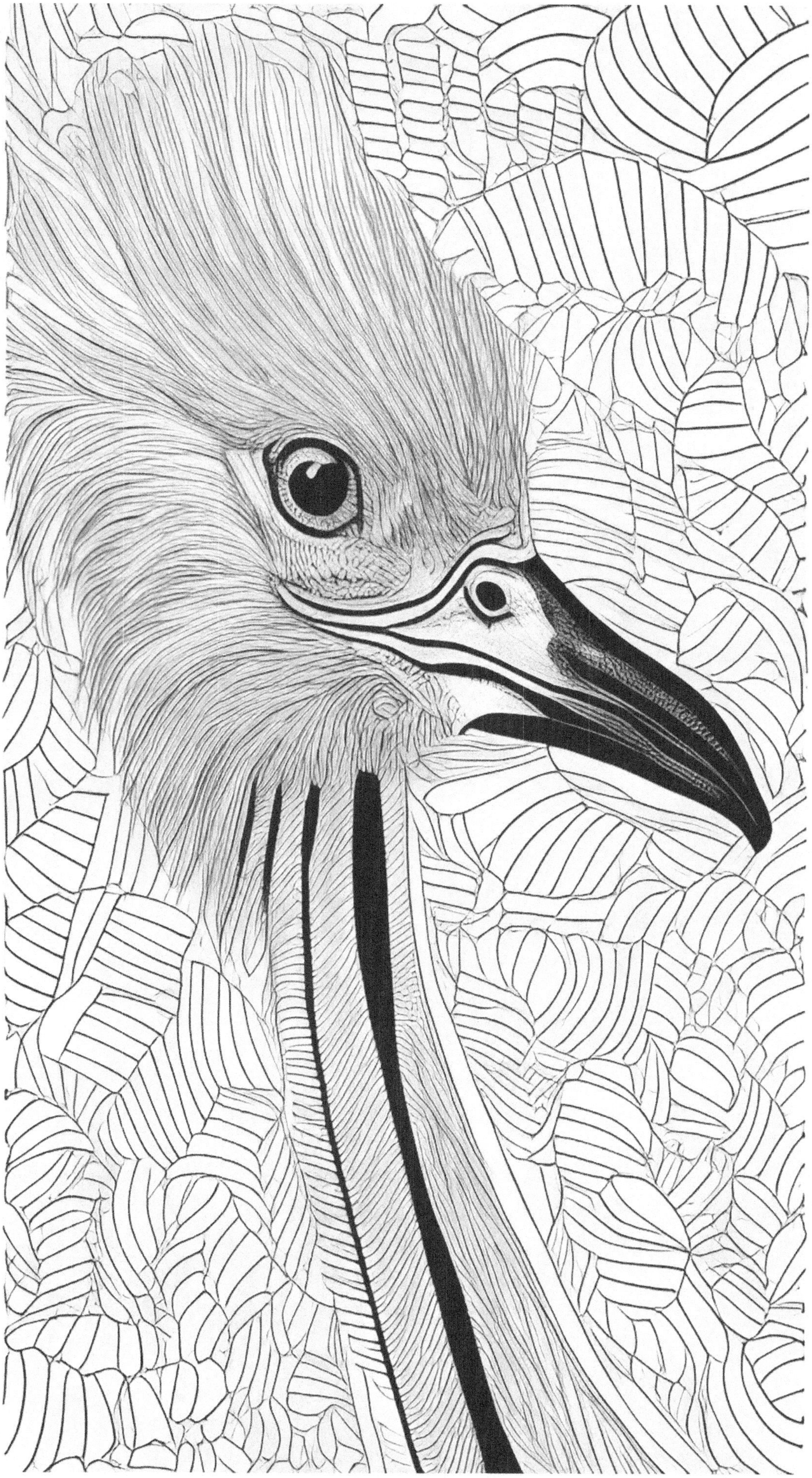

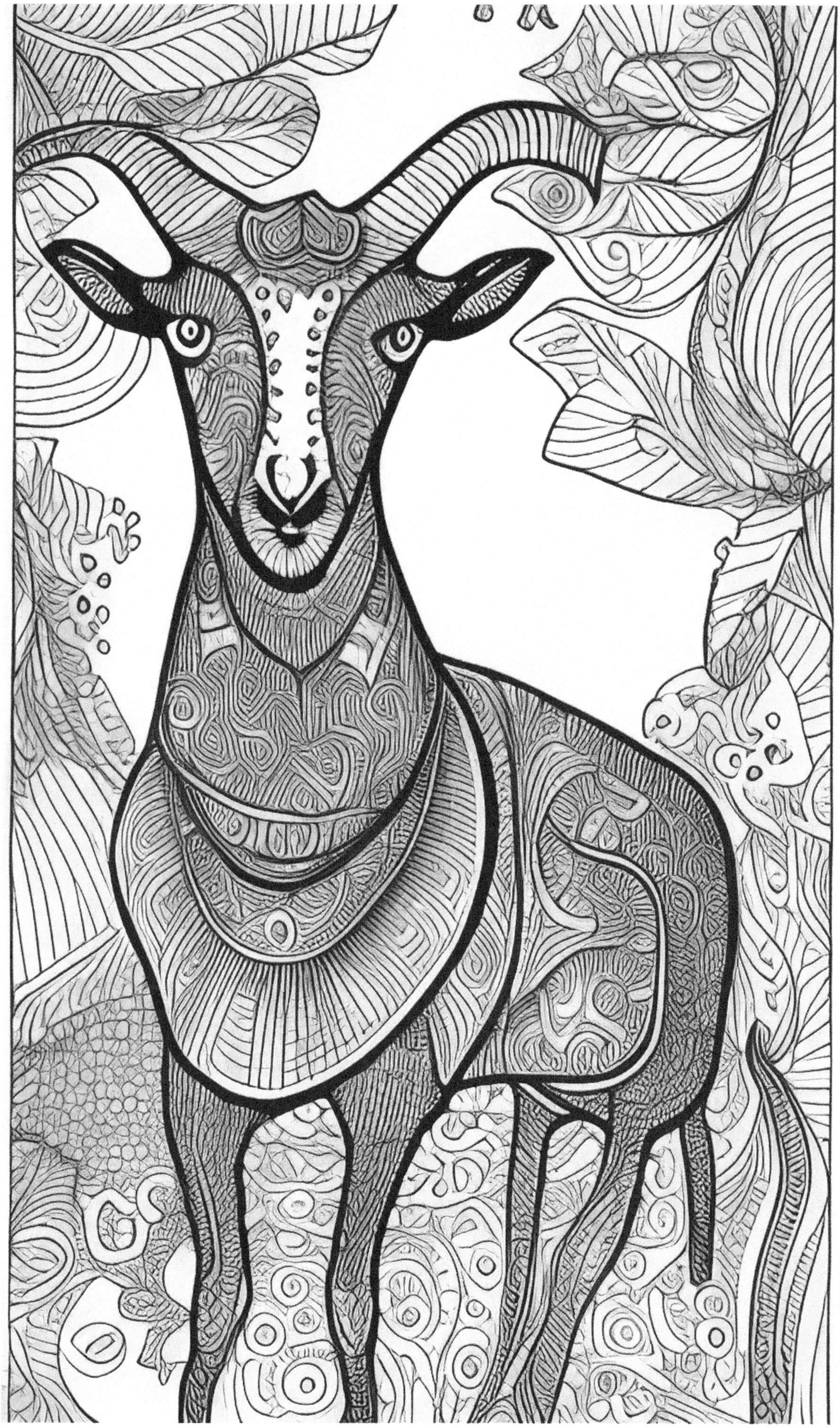

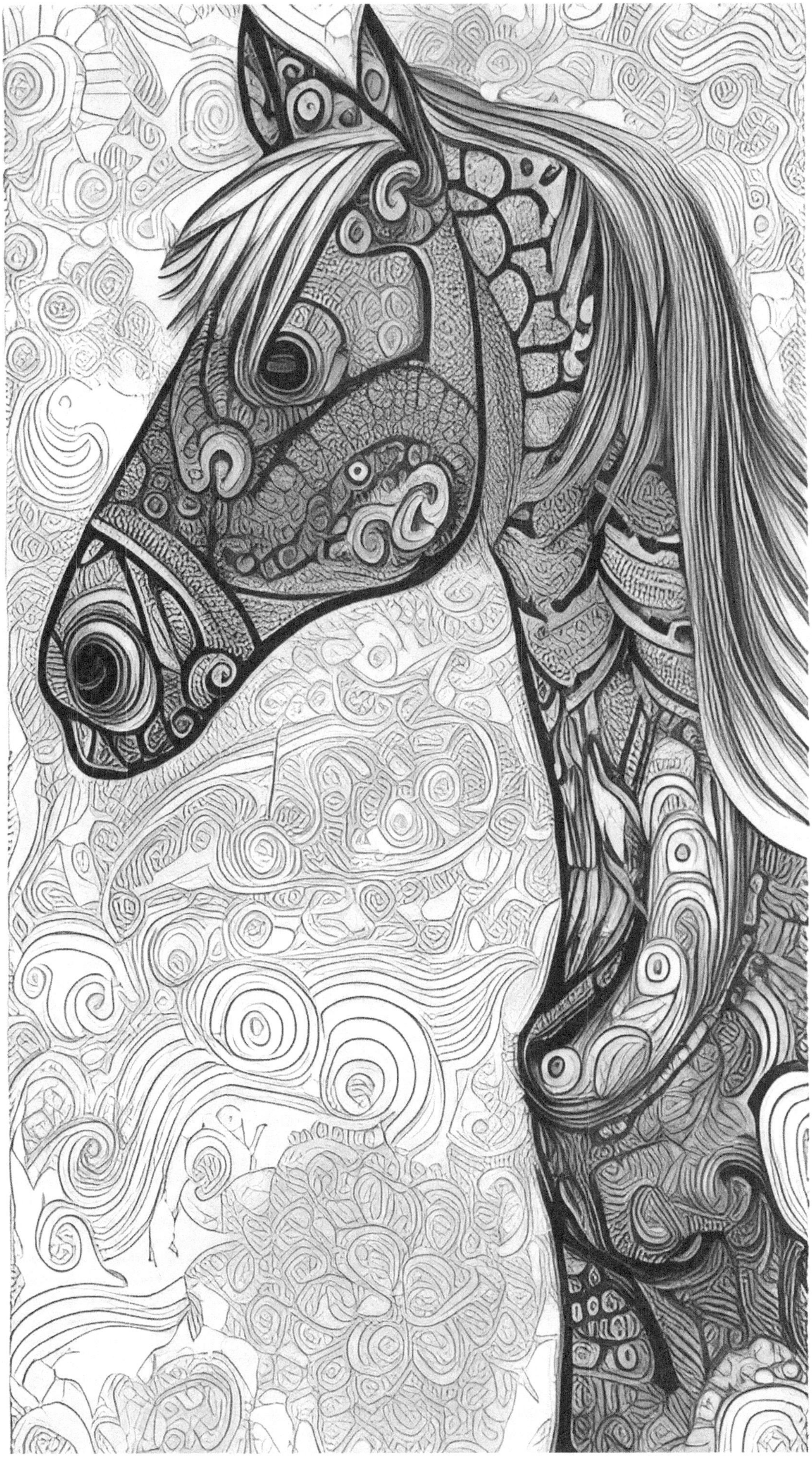

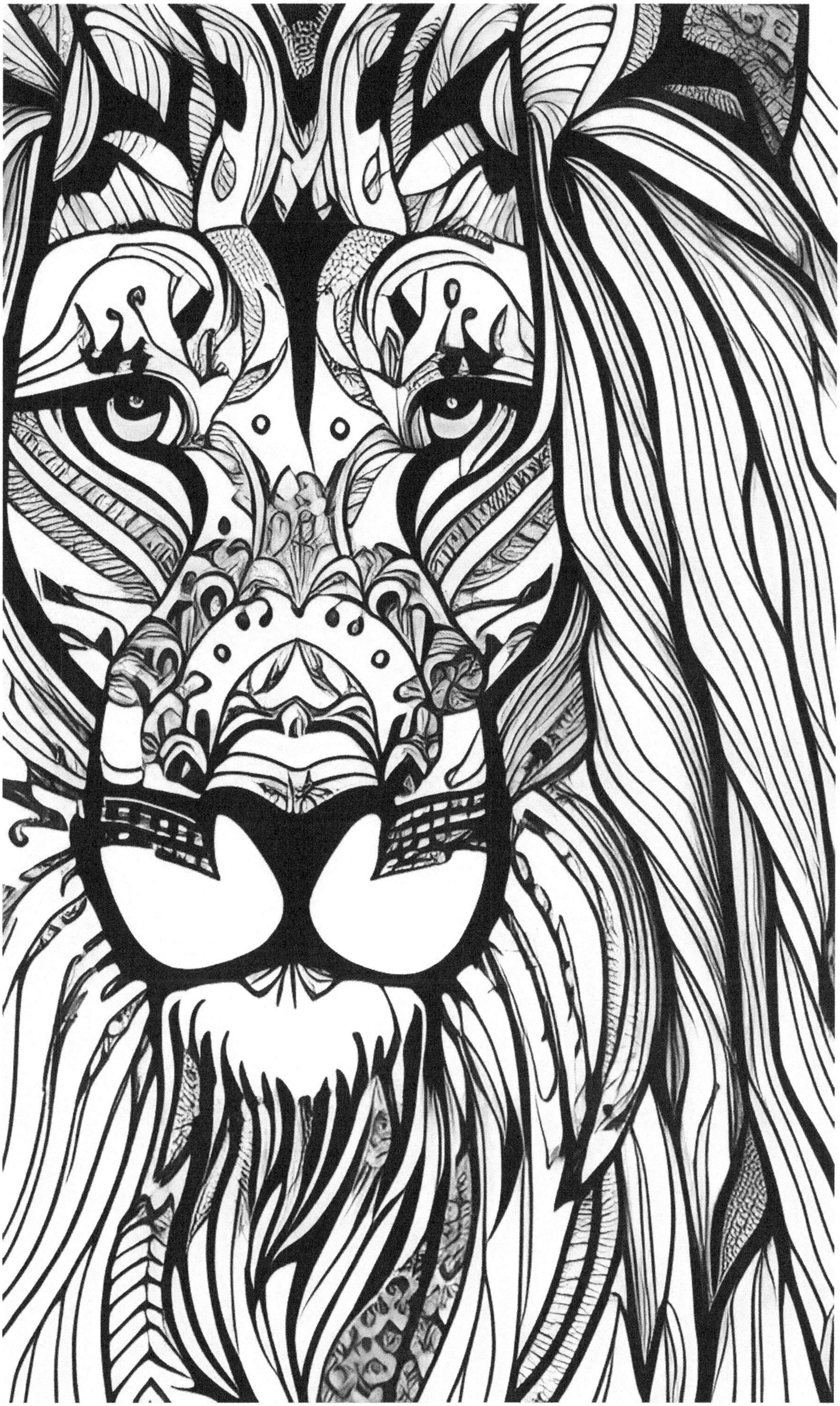

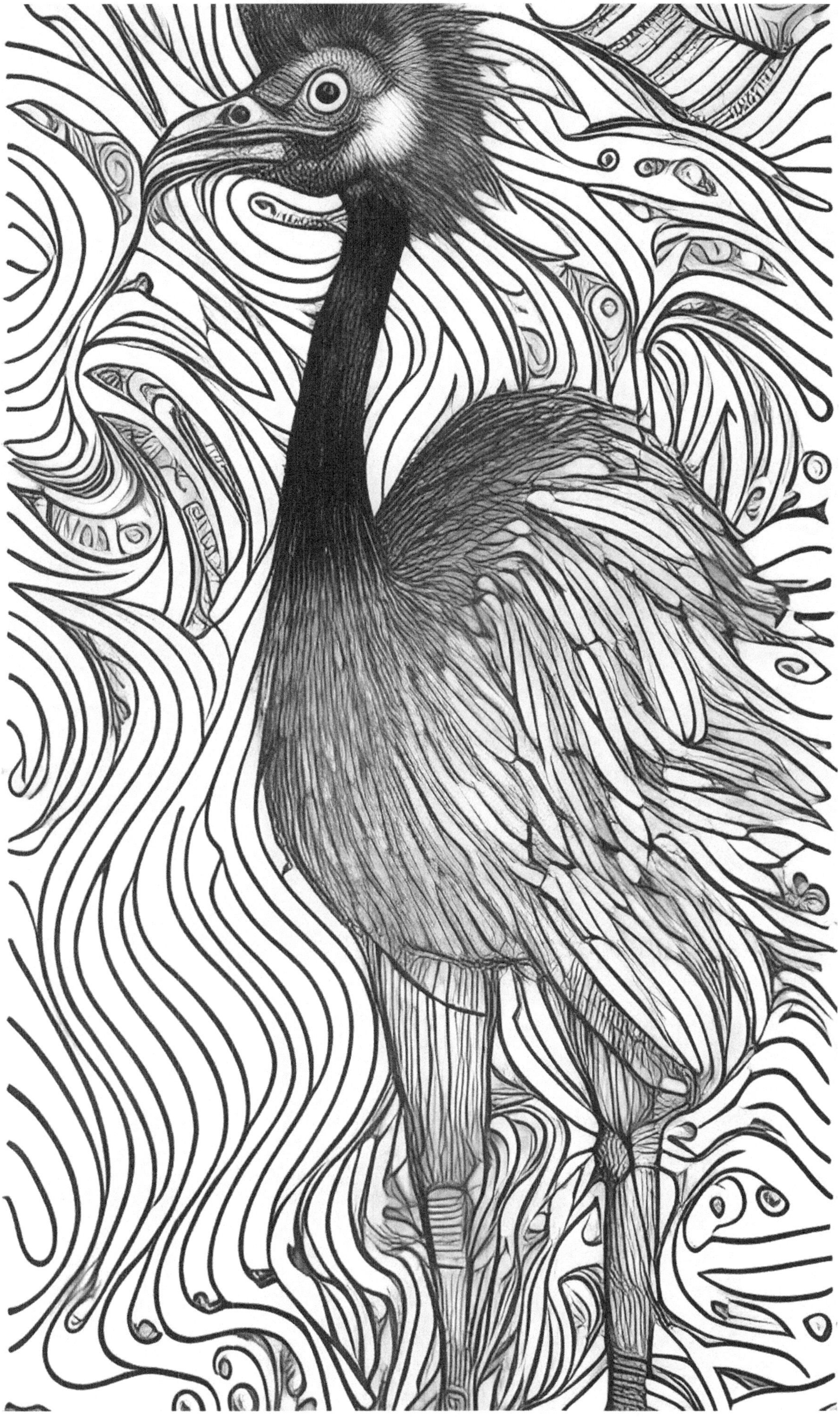

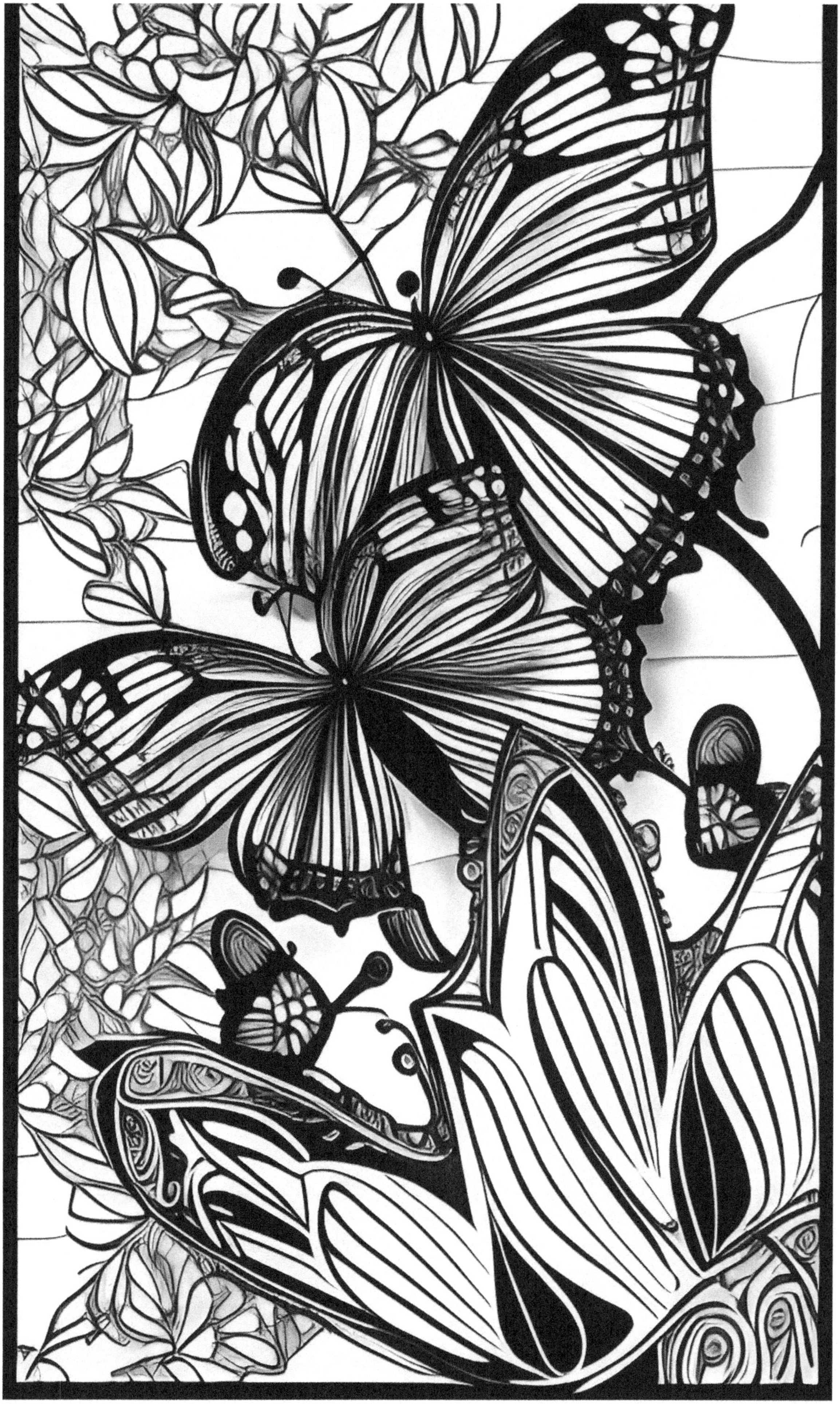

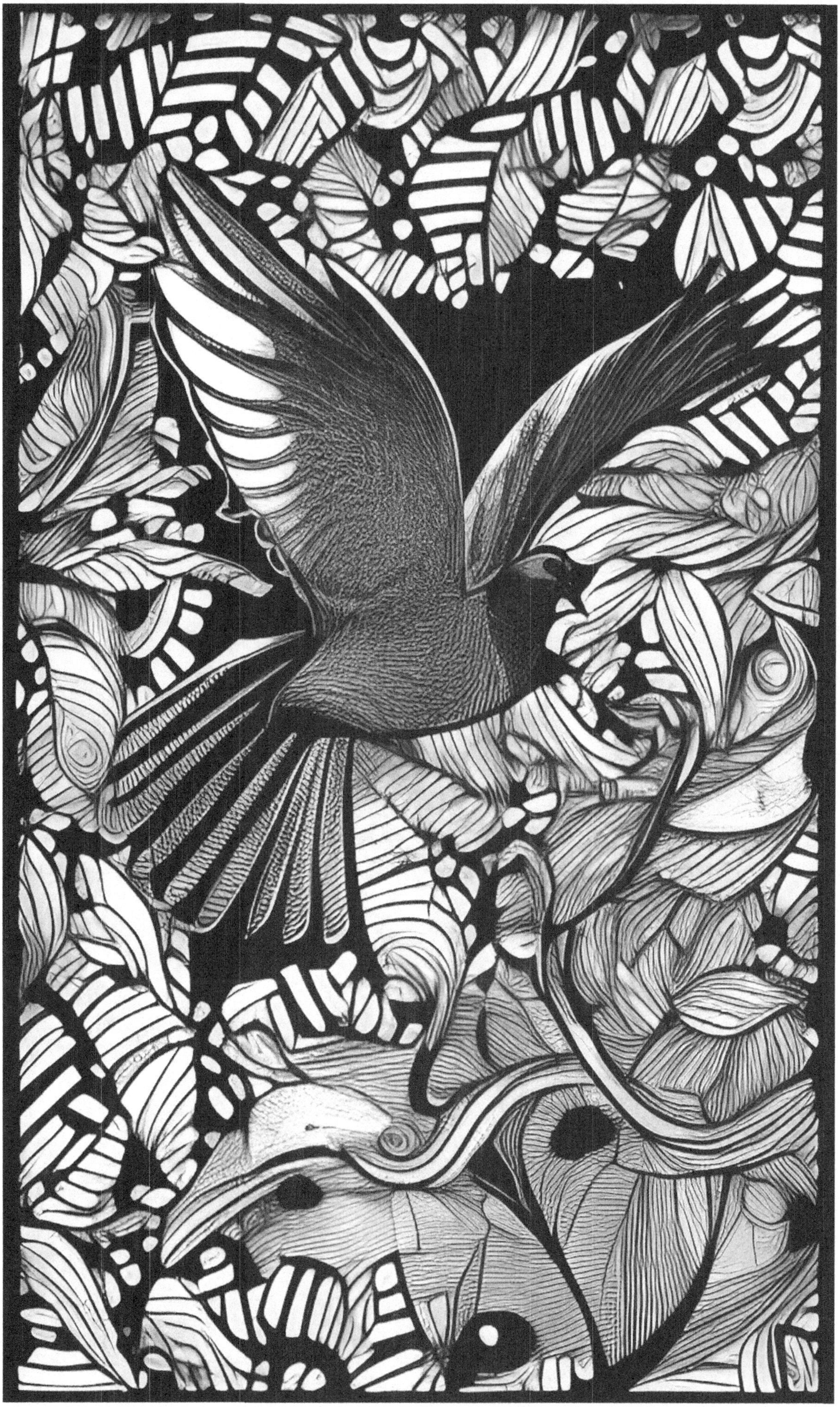

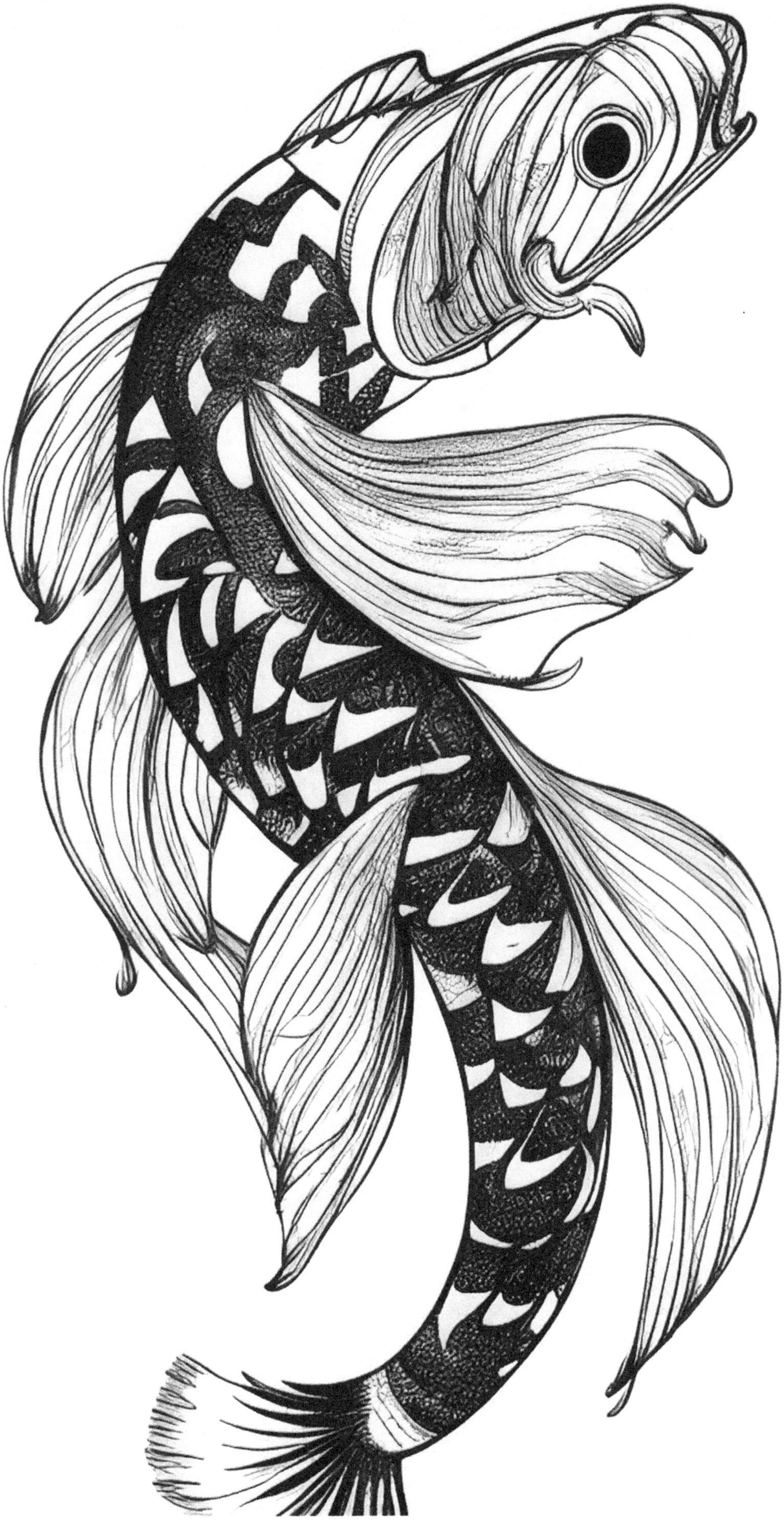

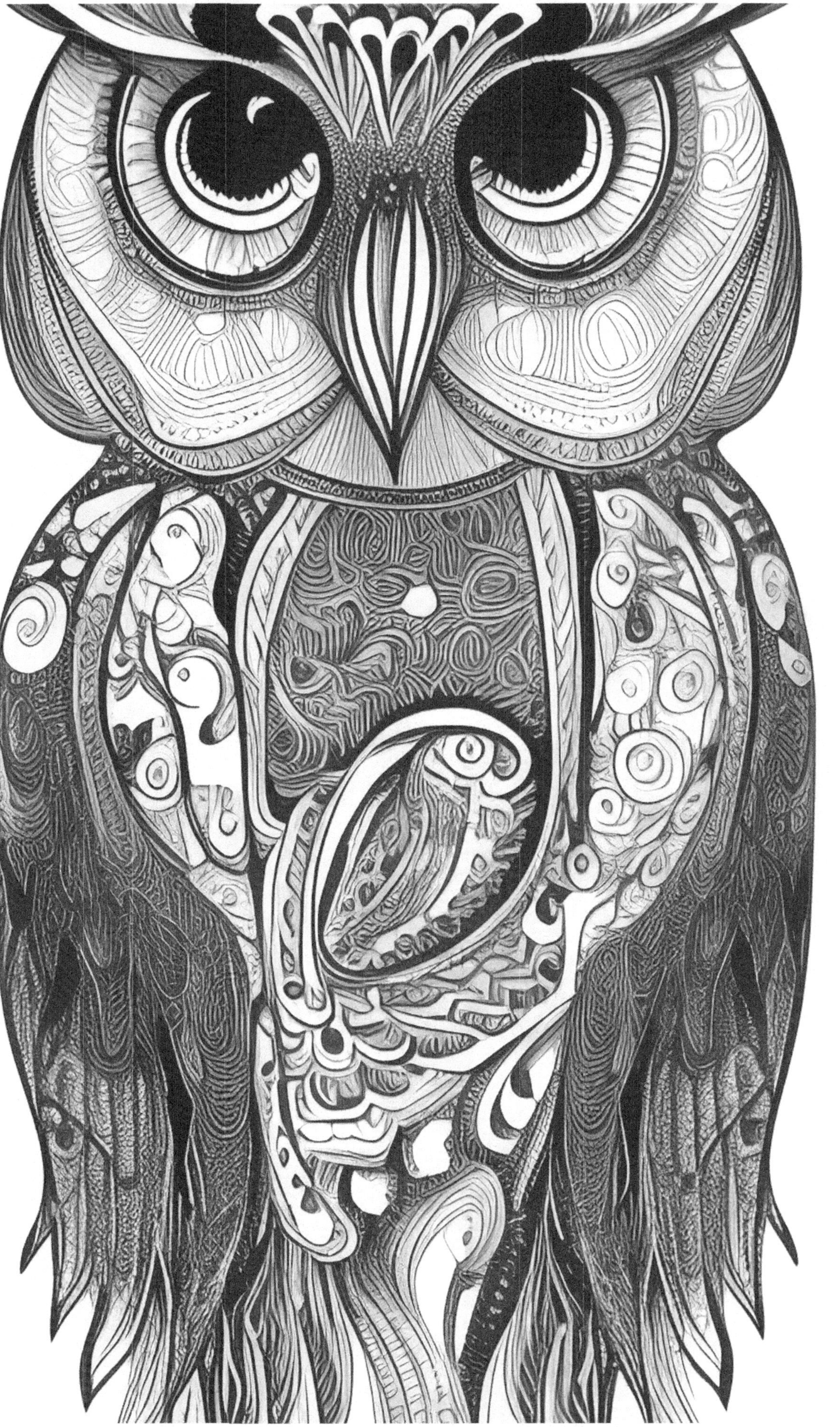

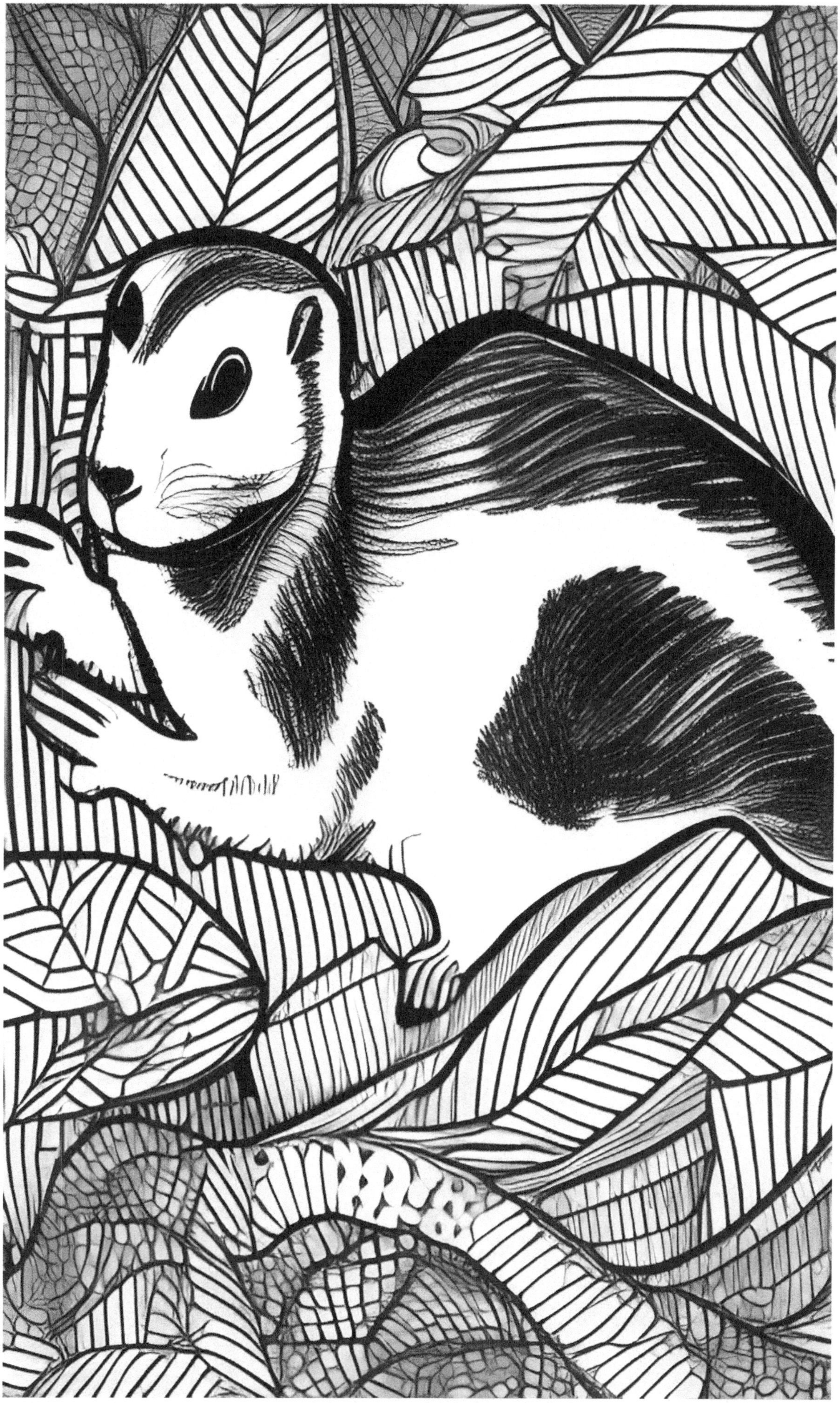

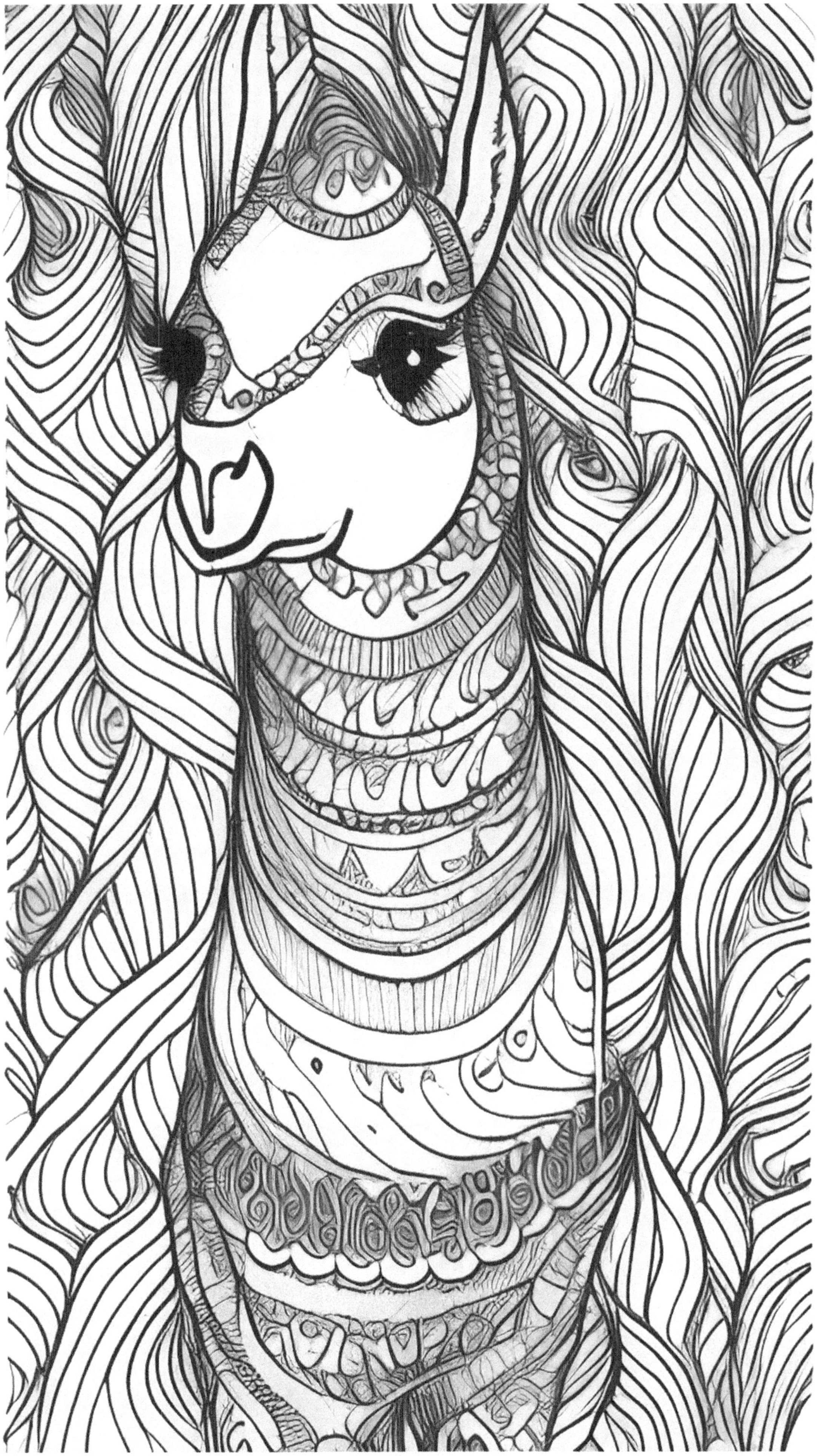

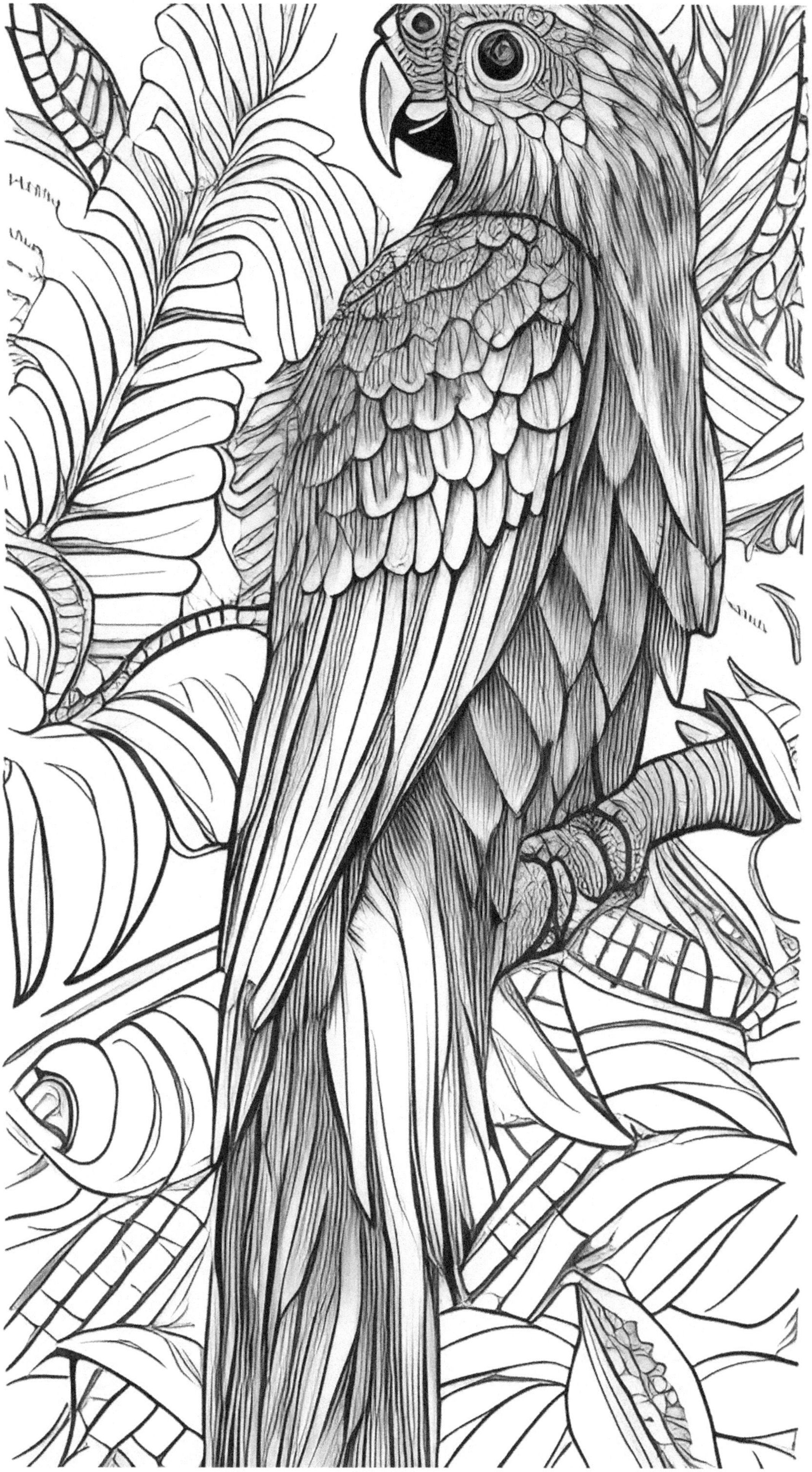

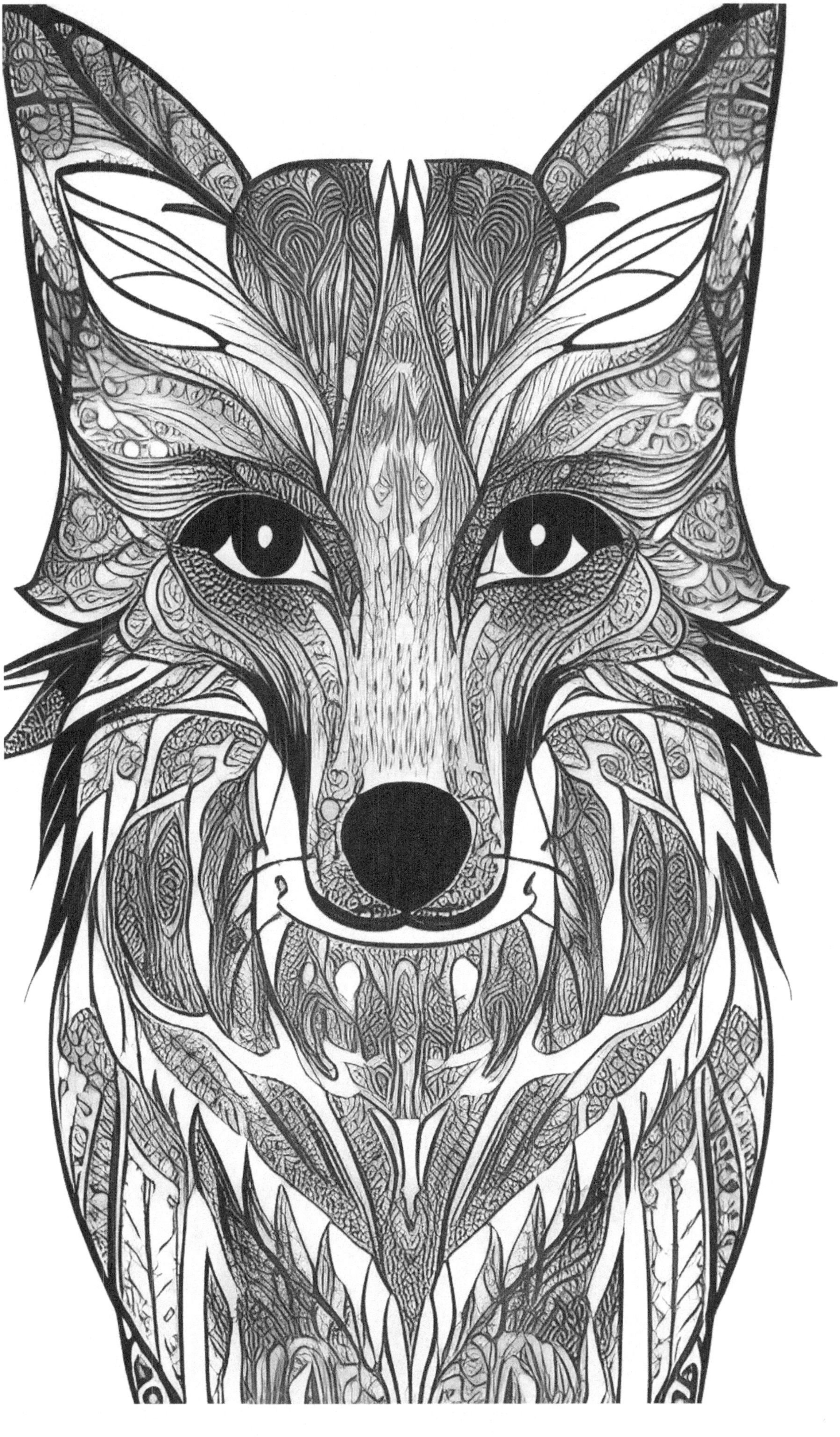

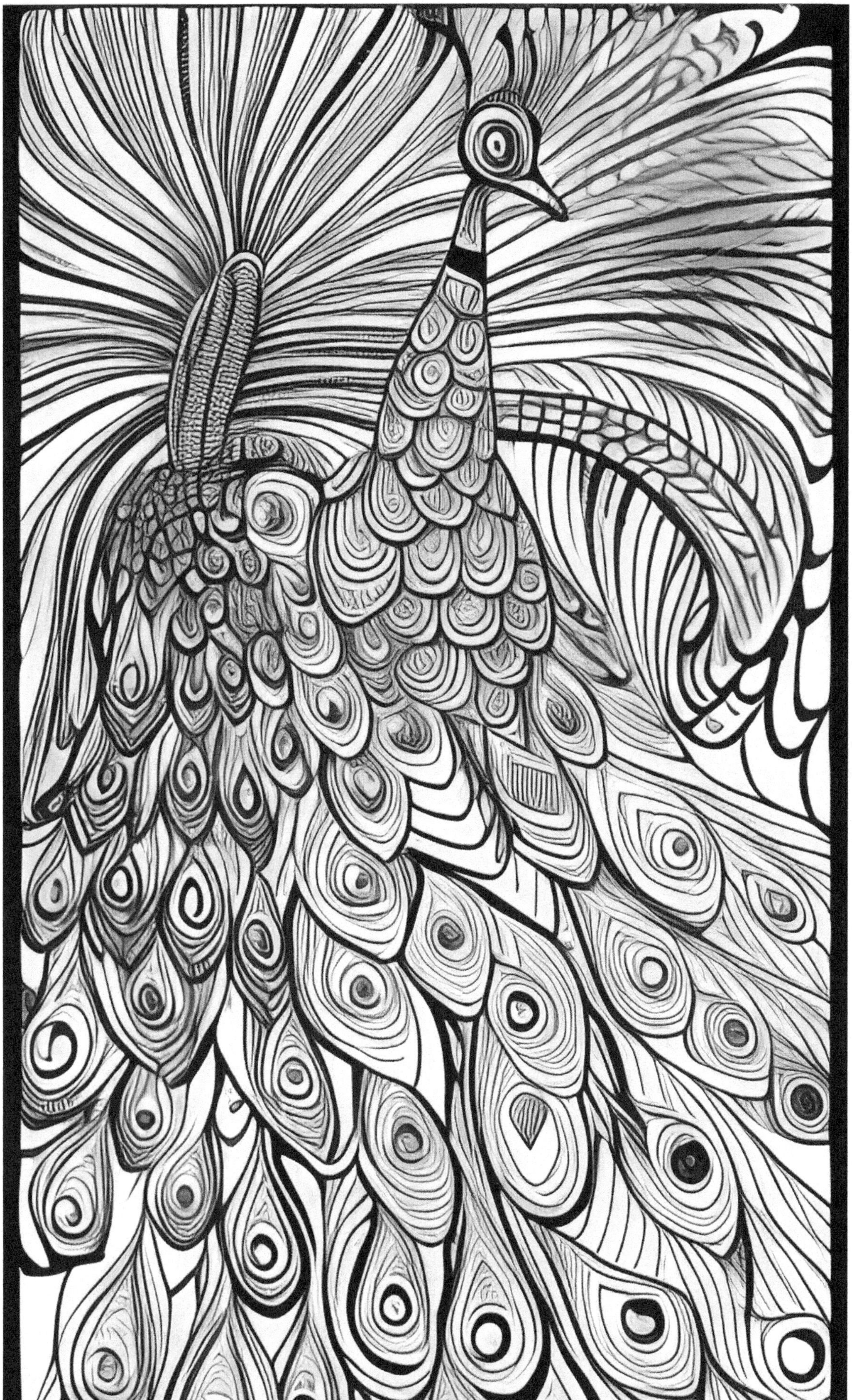

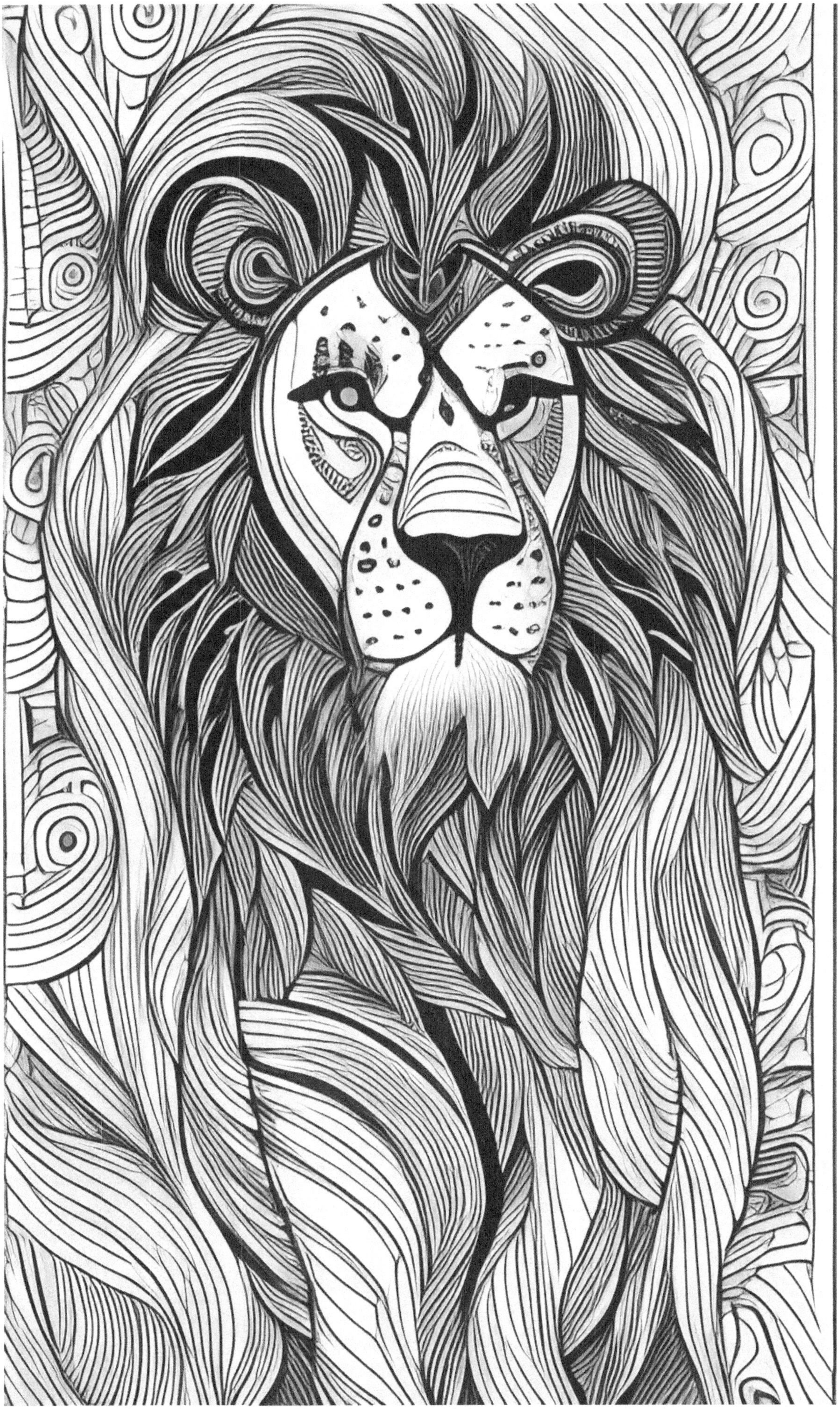

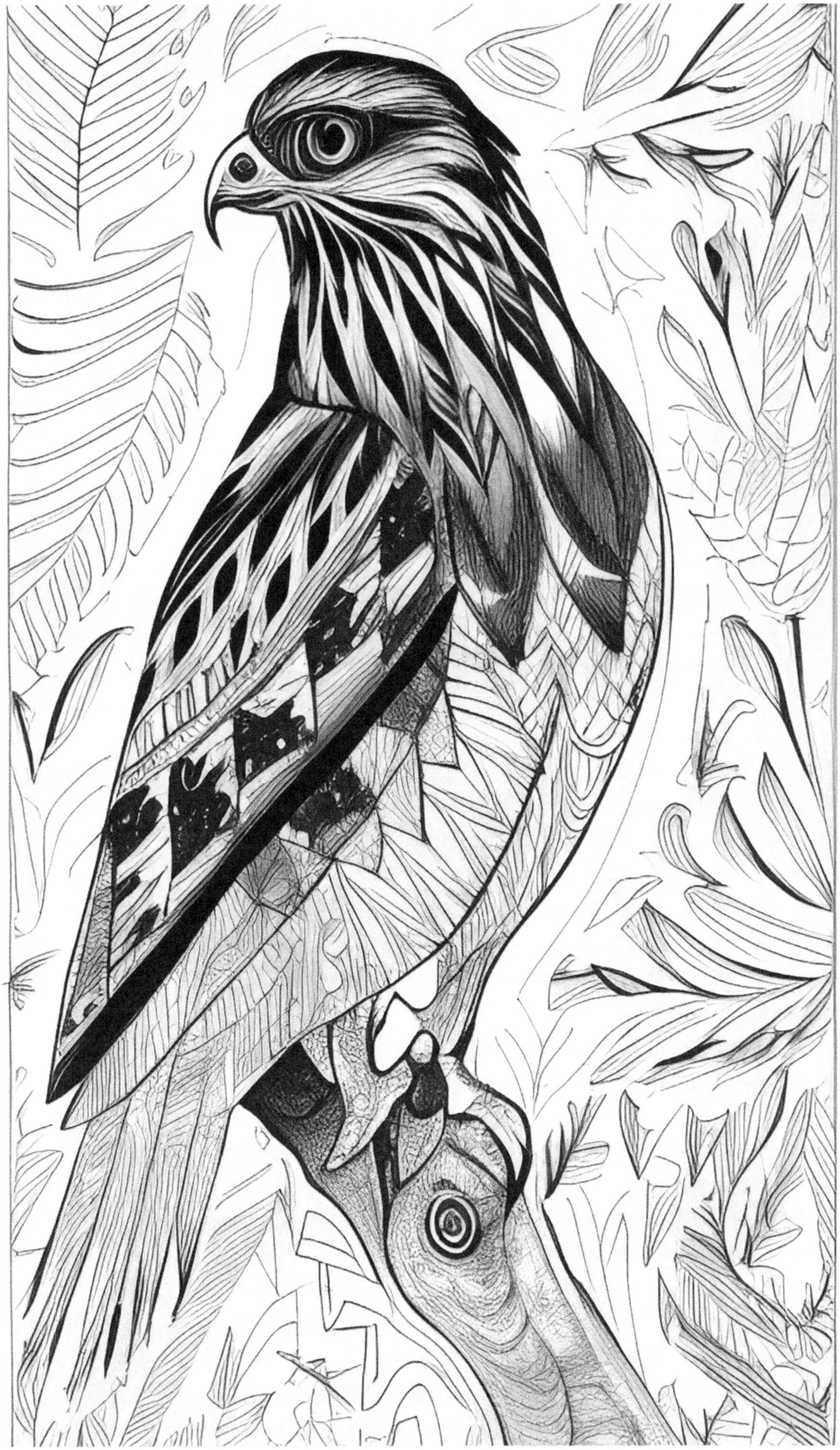

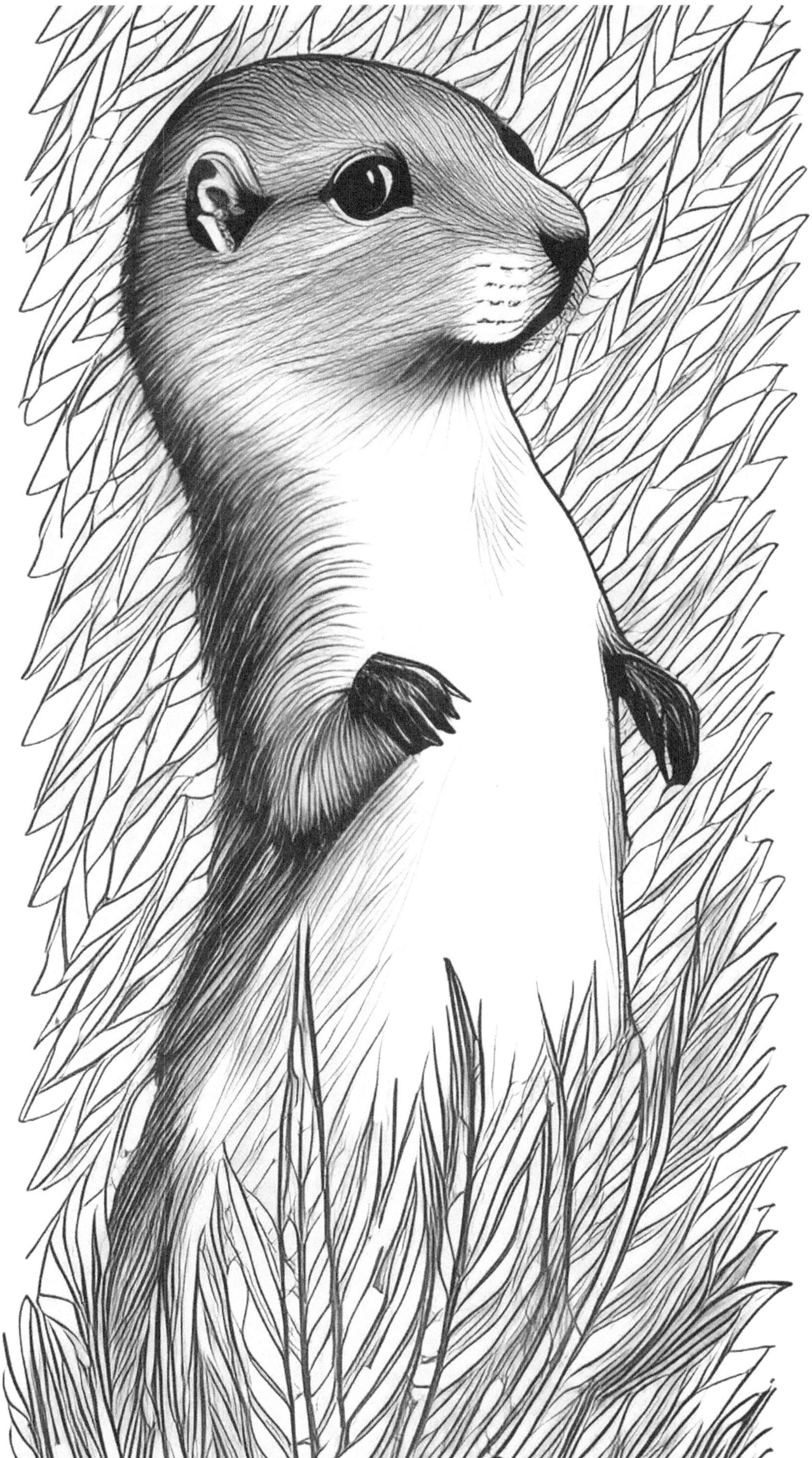

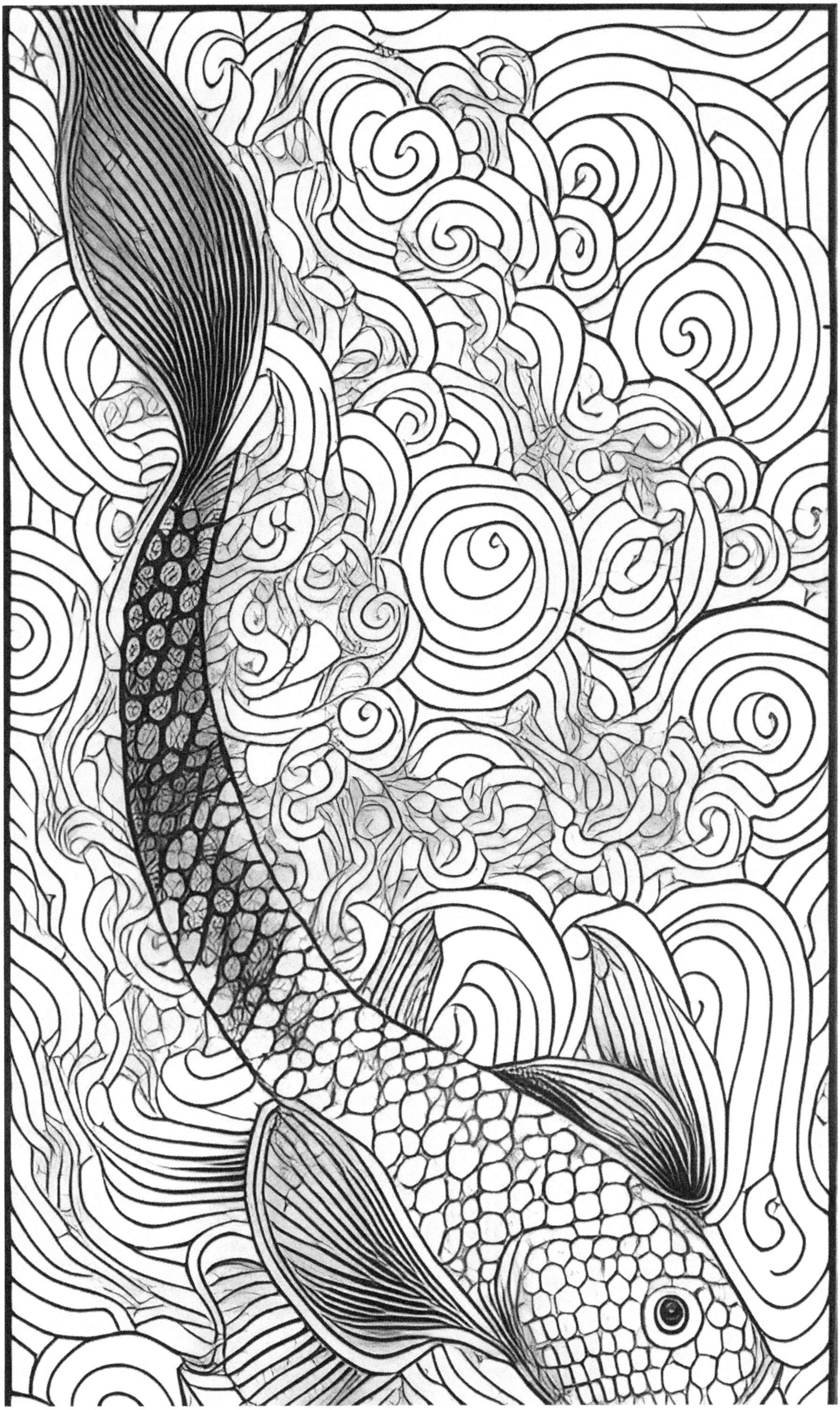

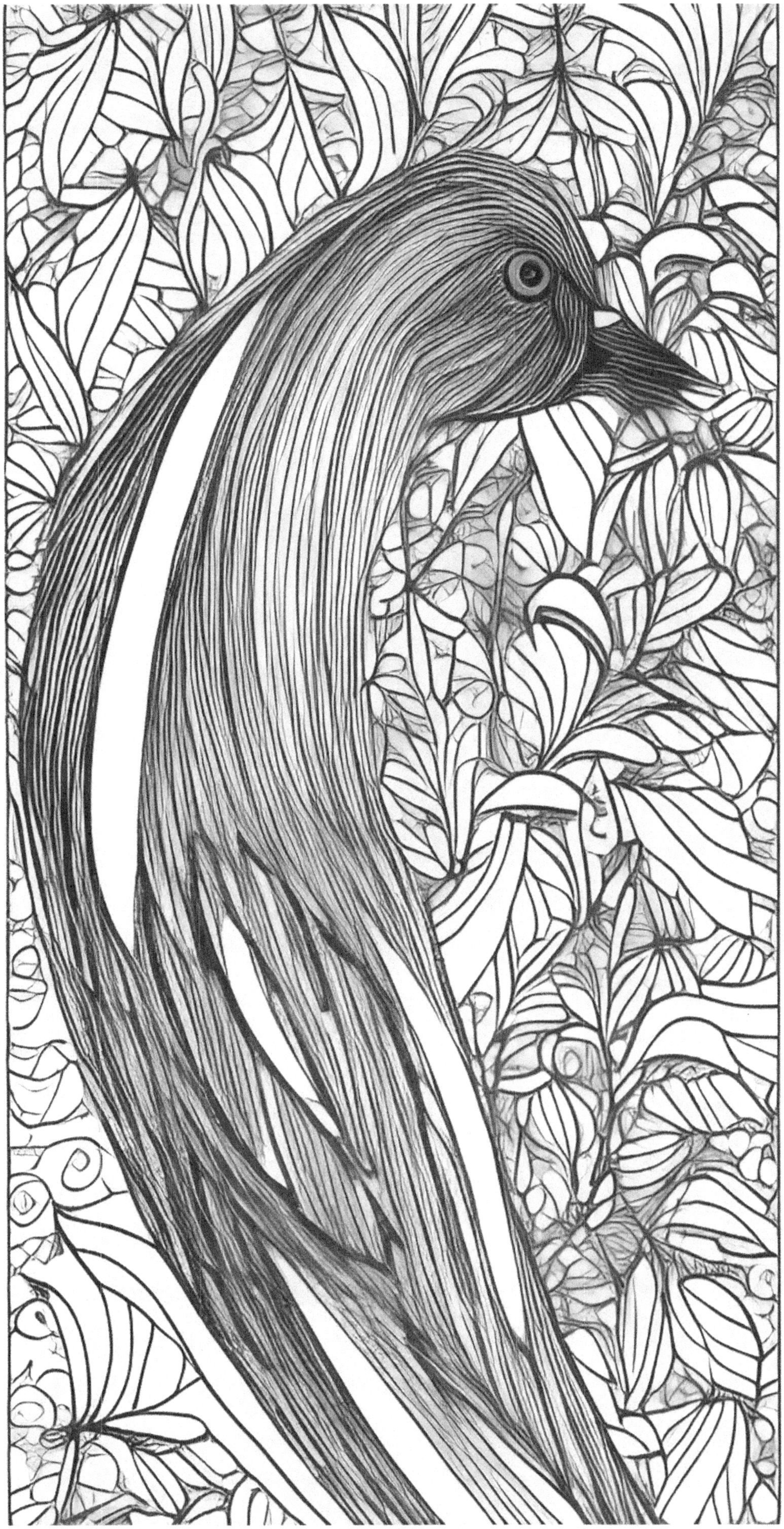

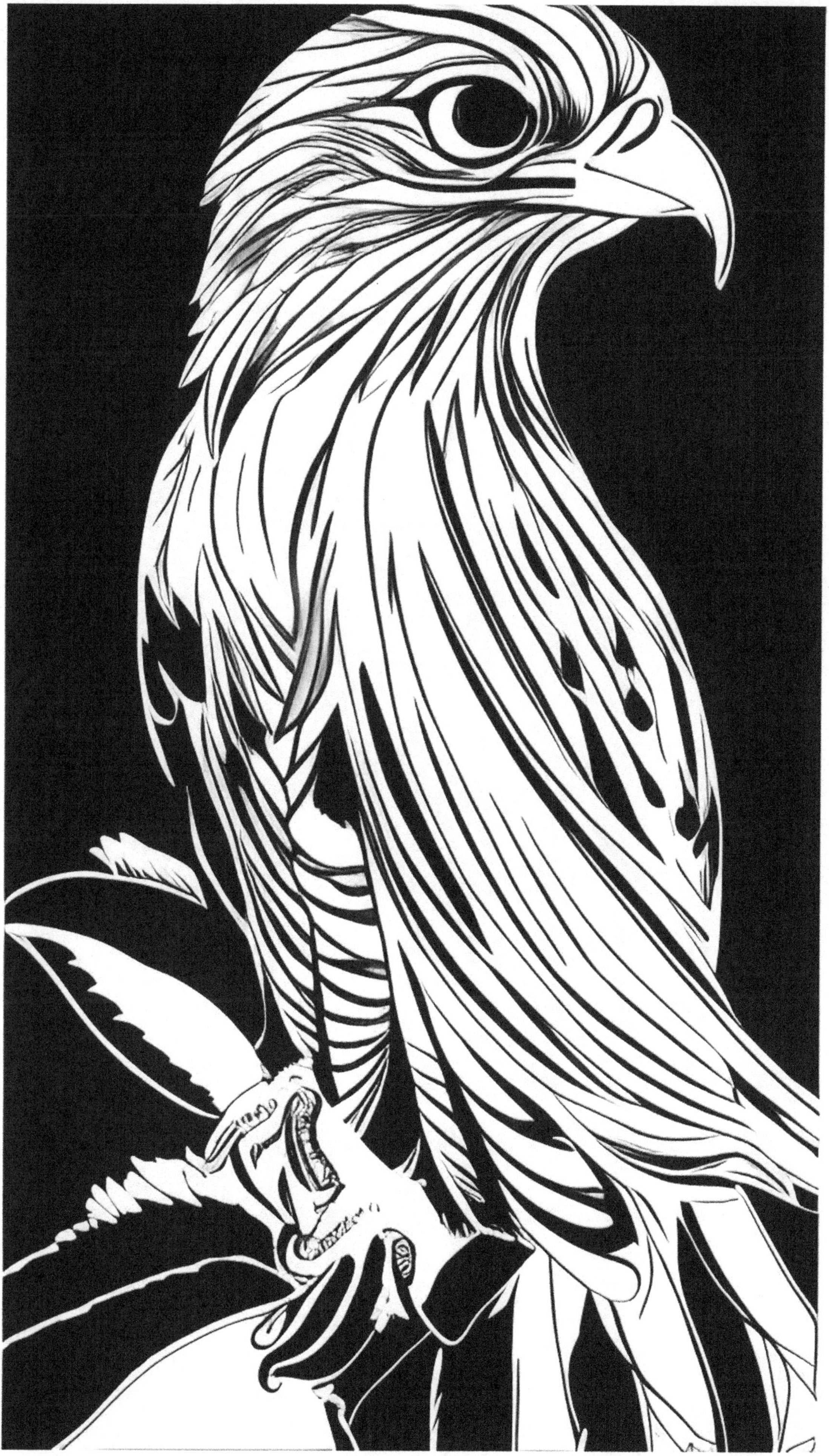

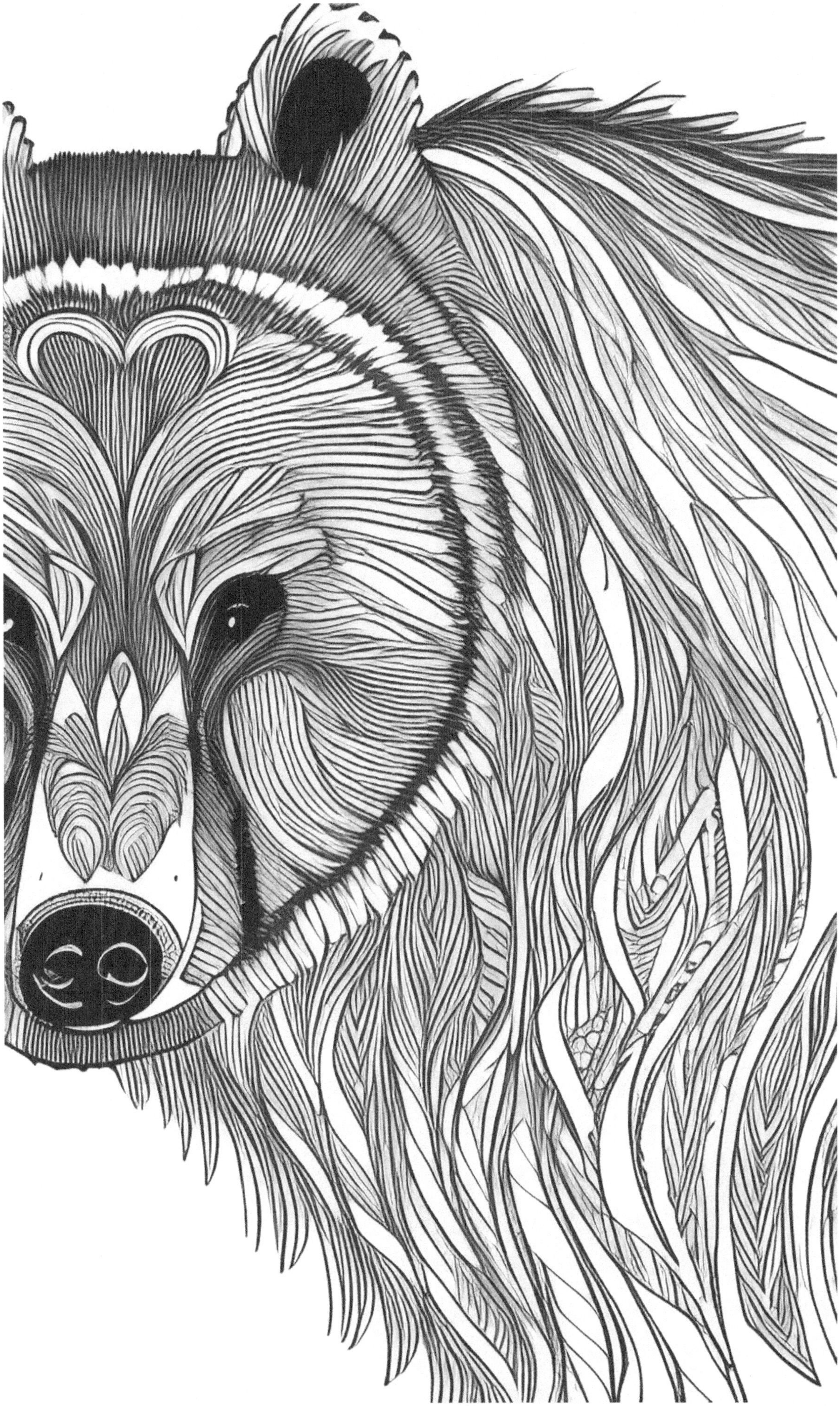

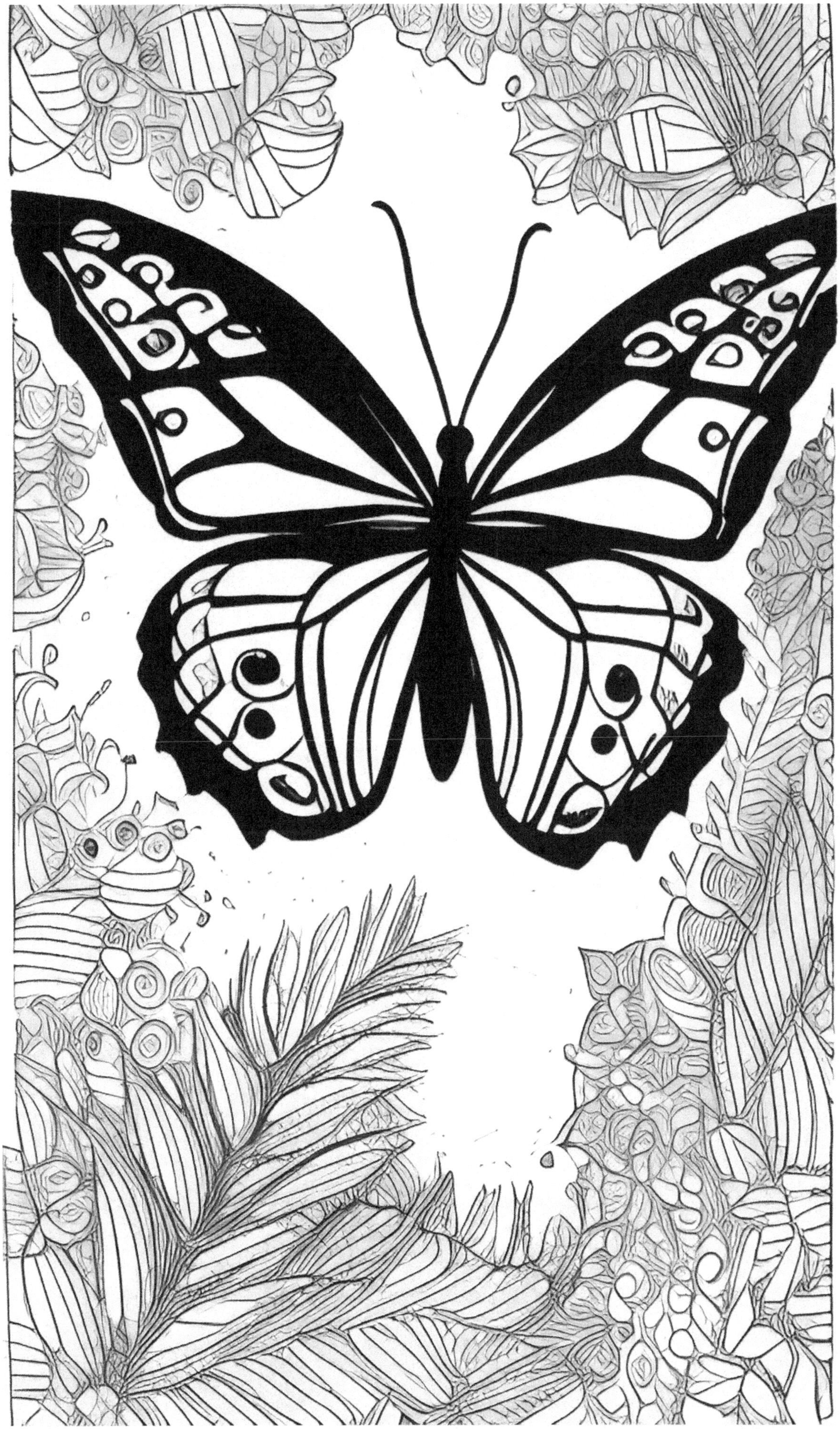

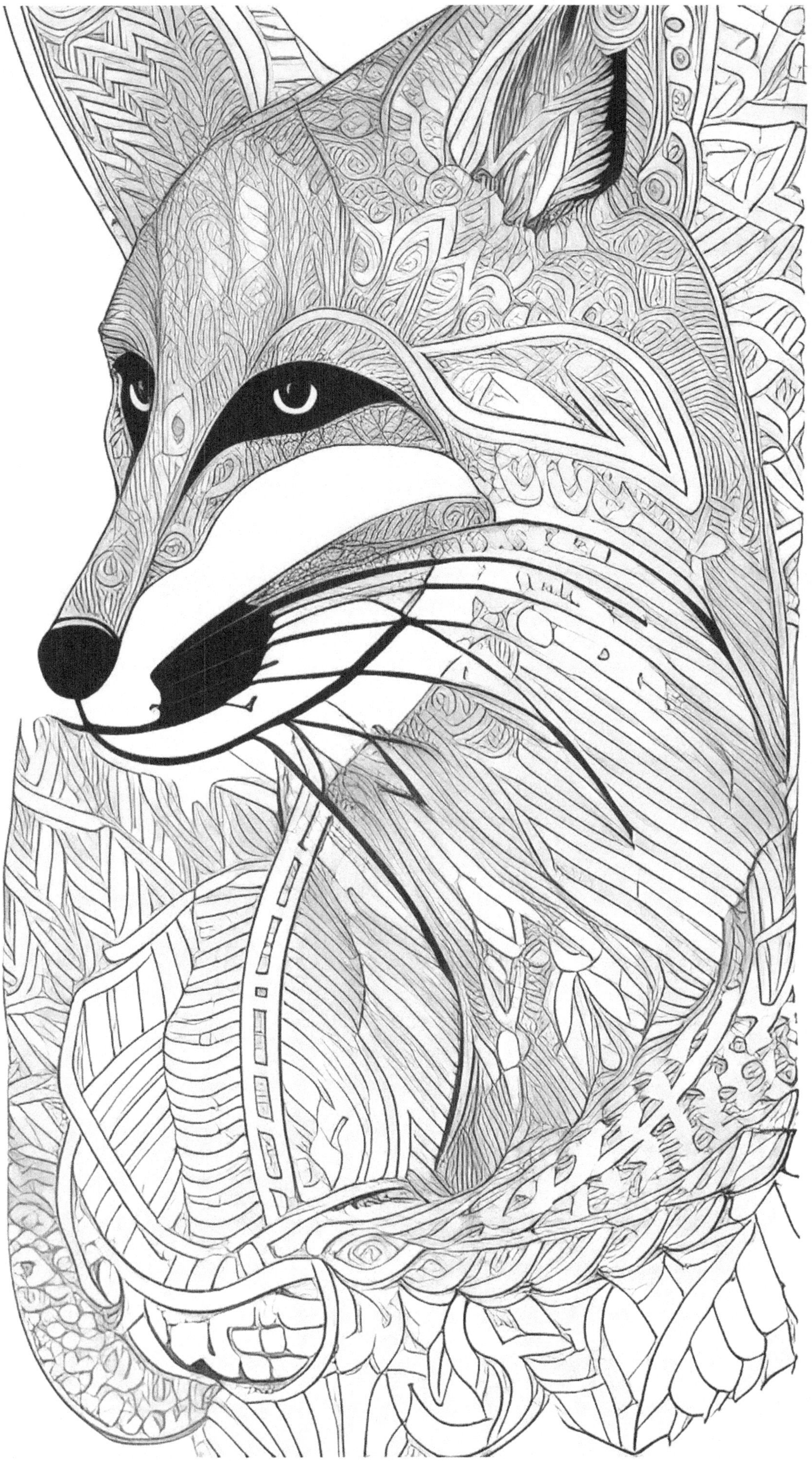

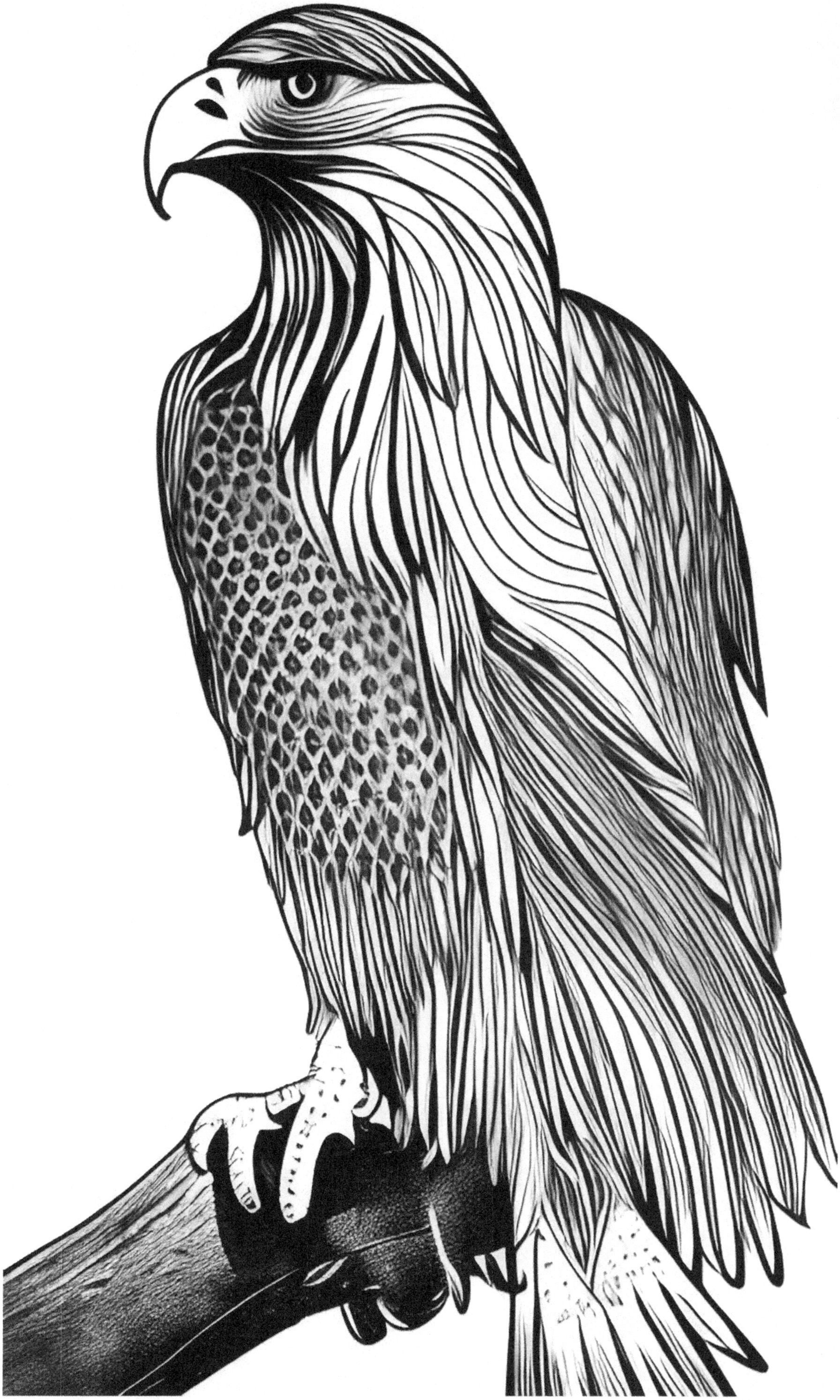

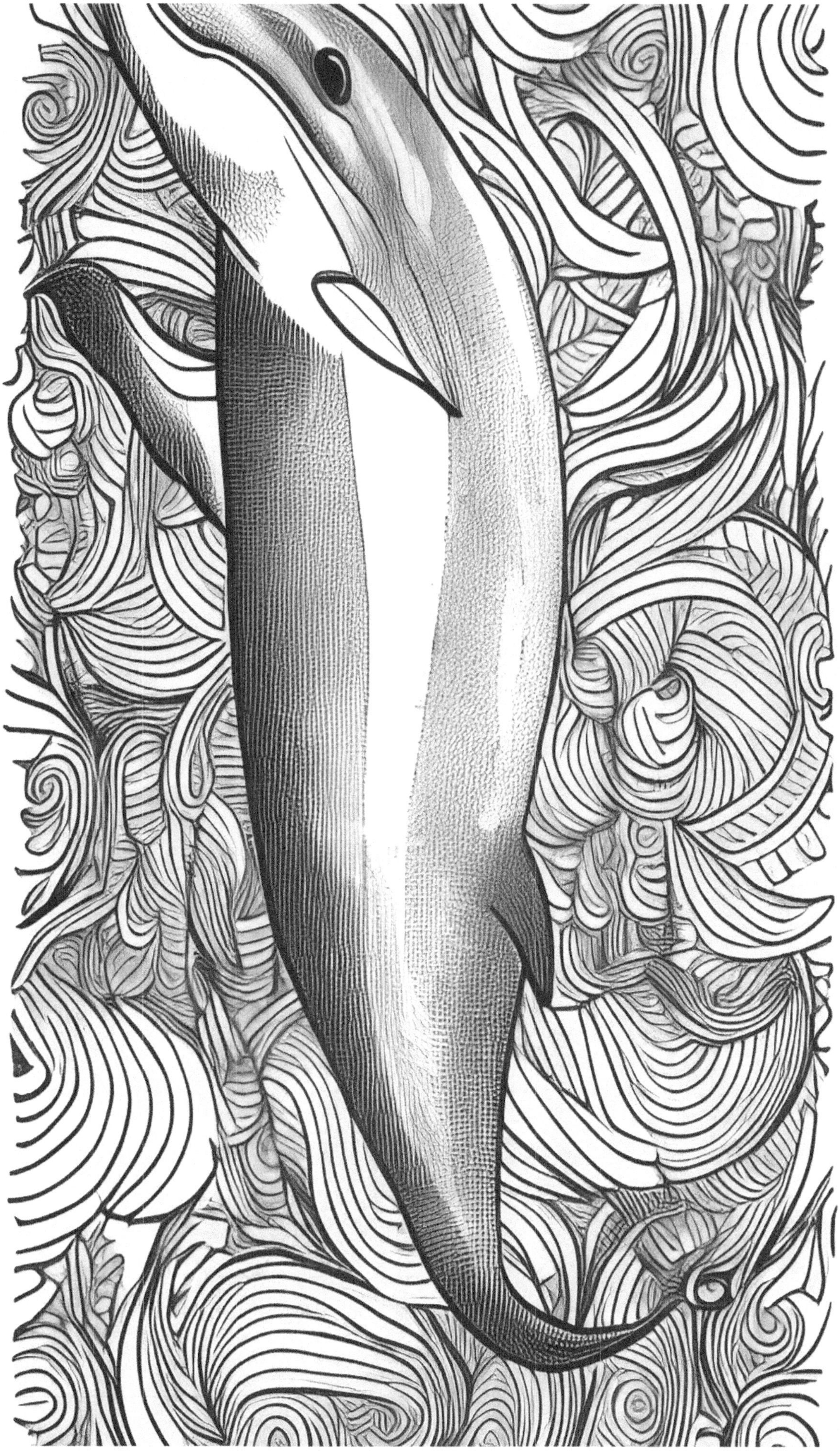

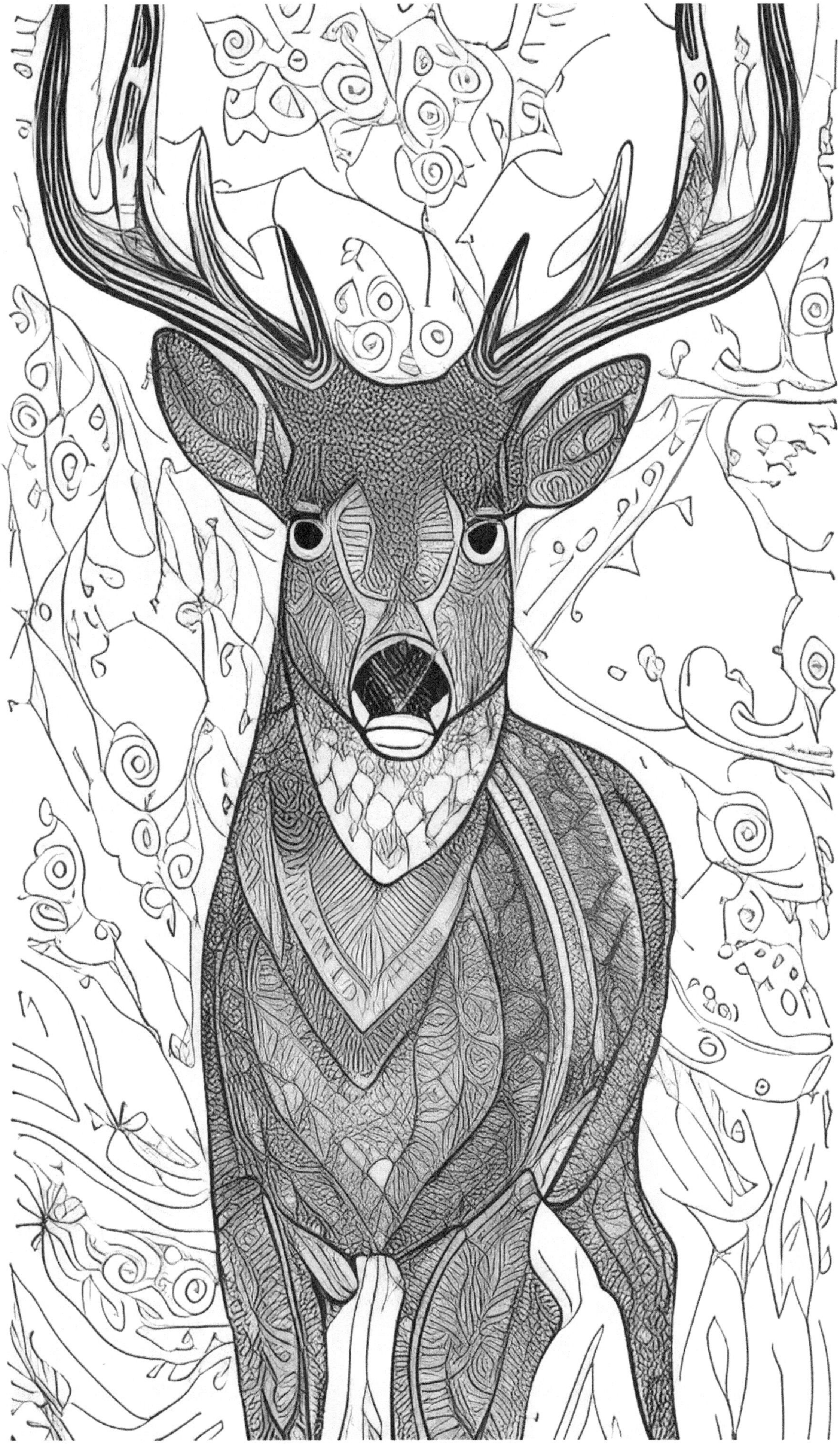

Made in the USA
Middletown, DE
09 April 2023

28422590R00051